1

To Sleep: Perchance to Dream - Shakespeare

THE ROLLING MOON

⌂ A journey to understand alien abduction ⌂

by

CAROL MELBER

⌐

This book is dedicated to family and friends for their support of the creative arts and to all who dare to dream.

Contents

		Page
	Dedication	4
	Introduction	6
Chapter		
1	When They Come	7
2	The Early Connection	17
3	Awakening Senses	26
4	Understanding Meditation	34
5	The Third Eye	41
6	Spontaneity	47
7	Instinct	52
8	The Coordinates	61
9	Angel Dog	68
10	The Return	72
11	The Transport	78
12	Communication	82
13	Evolution	90
14	The New Ones	94
15	Nine Lives	100
16	The Rolling Moon	115
	Epilogue	121
	References	122

Introduction

Normal: 1) an adjective-conforming to the standard or the common type; usual; not abnormal; regular; natural; average intelligence; free from mental disorder. 2) A noun-one that is normal; a form or state regarded as the norm. The state of normalcy changes in accordance with historical events, new discoveries, creative expression, and evolving ecosystems that shape our environment. Change in and of itself is normal because nothing is constant, whatever the form, it is always in a state of change.

If we accept as the norm the premiss that UFO's do not exist to reach a conclusion that no alien lifeforms have ever visited Planet Earth we close out the possibility of other means of travel and overlook the percentage of UFO sightings that have not been explained. New discoveries made in outer space exploration and research have uncovered evidence of alien life, lending credence to the nonconformist theory that we are not alone in this universe. Considering the vast number of galaxies in the universe it is rather absurd to think that our solar system, one of 500 identified and 10 billion estimated in the Milky Way Galaxy alone, is the only one that includes a planet with the perfect conditions to sustain intelligent life. It simply does not make logical sense.

This book captures the lifetime journey of one person who opens her mind to the probability that we are not alone in the universe and her struggle to understand the mystery of alien abduction. It contains historical facts and is based on actual events, all of which were normal to her. It is all she knew.

Chapter One
When They Come
◯

The fog will settle in thick tonight, she thinks to herself while on a late afternoon jog. It is already rolling through the valley toward the ridge-top. Her vantage point at the top of the ridge provides a spectacular view. She can see the natural valley line below and beyond the few remaining working ranches. Terraced hillsides are etched on both sides with unique landscape designs that trim the oversized houses tucked inside gated communities developed to provide the residents both privacy and optimum view of the hills, each appearing to slightly overlap the one before, and all sloping inward and into the same valley that disappears westward into the glistening waters of the Pacific. When the fog rolls in from the ocean it always rolls up the same path, through the valley, up to the ridge-top where it appears to linger, as if it is surveying the subdivision below before it widens then makes its descent. It won't be long before it blankets the entire subdivision in its cool heavy mist. When the fog rolls in from the ocean it moves purposefully, unlike the drop of low-lying clouds that flirtatiously rise and fall in random places during a rainfall or in the early hours of dawn. Rolling fog is not random at all and it is never teasing. Rolling fog is steady, deliberate, and serious. As she jogs along it occurs to her that in this exact moment she is preparing. Her mind is preparing for what surely will follow later in the night, and she is not afraid. At this realization she feels a sense of extreme clarity, like after a weather front blows through, removes stagnant pollutants, leaving the air clear. Visibility is at a maximum then and everything you see looks crisp and in focus. Her sense of clarity quickly transcends into an almost mundane awareness as she thinks, "Oh yeah, it's that time, again." She feels just as she did as a child on Sunday mornings when she was told it was time to get ready for church. She knew it was coming, was not particularly thrilled about it, but deep inside she also knew she would feel uplifted afterward.

The sun is setting and is no longer visible at the western horizon, now completely blanketed by fog. The daylight remaining is now shadowed by the hills and large homes peppering each side of string after string of cul-de-sacs. She looks up at the sky and sees the light quickly changing from shades of blue twilight to a darker grey as the enveloping fog continues its pursuit. It is moving along faster now and will be thickly surrounding the townhouse by the time she jogs back to the bottom of the hill. As she continues the decline she breathes in the damp air deeply and notices the glow of a streetlamp below as it captures the swirling, spiral movement of the fog that is rapidly descending upon the village. Her townhouse, second in a row of four, faces the frontage road and south. The rows of townhouses vary from three to four and are situated along the frontage road and behind, nestled in clusters around weaving streets that all end in cul-de-sacs.

The development is one of those very well planned, backing up to nature type projects. The green areas, walkways, play areas, clubhouses, paths, and sidewalks are all strategically placed to maximize space or enhance the esthetic value of the development, a 'Green Development'-the latest trend in environment friendly living. Green developments recycle drain run off for watering, encourage trash recycling and provide residents with a purchase option of a convenient means of electric transportation, similar to the electric carts maneuvering the narrow paths of most golf courses. Each unit is outfitted with the proper plug outlet in the garage and on any given day you can see these carts motoring on the bike paths around the development. She did not go 'electric cart green' but did have extra energy efficient features built into the townhouse. From the windows to air filtering system, her home was built to green standards and the proof it worked appeared in the utility bills. She had a fifty percent reduction in energy cost even though her townhouse was over 900 square feet larger than her previous apartment rental. Green rules!

As she jogs she thinks about the grueling process she went through to win her option to purchase the lot and build her home. The shortage of land available to develop coupled with an ever-increasing population demanding housing resulted in a list and lottery purchasing system. Anyone who wanted to purchase attended open house events in order to get their names on builder lists. Each new phase opening announced the names of those fortunate enough to purchase before the next phase and inevitable price increase. She was priced out of two developments before she won her option to purchase a lot and build. She thinks about the weekend visits to the site during construction, taking pictures to memorialize the progress. She remembers the long list of decisions she made on materials, color-schemes, and extras. She remembers the triumphant feeling she had while the movers were unloading the furniture she bought while still living at the apartment that was, in the end, crammed tightly with pieces too large for its size. She remembers the glow on her daughter's smiling face, lit by the flames of the gas fireplace ablaze and spreading warmth across the living room as she watched the movers unload their possessions. She remembers feeling a sense of pride in her ownership and in herself. She remembers feeling a sense of belonging. This was her neighborhood, her stomping grounds, her sanctuary, her home, even if it was less than a stones throw away from her neighbor.

The builders adjusted for the proximity by assuring each unit was separate, so no shared walls, and they offset the postage size lots by building the homes higher, so a three story home with a garage and storage space below was the norm. The benefit of a high cost house in an over-crowded neighborhood is living in a safe, family oriented community with good schools, even if it is in a high fire risk area.

Subdivisions located near a National Forest or wild life preserves are designated as high fire risk. If you purchase a home in a high-risk area you are provided with a disclosure that you are required to sign at closing (like anyone is going to back out of the sale at that point). The high fire danger disclosure shows a topical map of the area dotted with tiny fire flame symbols that cover the fire danger area. Only after looking at such a map does one fully understand that there is not only the real danger of a fire because the land nearly surrounding where you live contains patches of wilderness or abuts a national forest, but there may be a limited number of escape routes if ever needed.

In her case there was one main road that ran north to south through the heart of the development. To reach her townhouse from that road she could take a winding canyon road in from the North or a steep declining road in from the South. Either route could be problematic in the event of a disaster for the simple reason that there were so many residents crammed in the development. The canyon road posed a particular problem because it acted as a wind tunnel. It was the main road in the development hosting blowing tumbleweeds during Santa Ana Wind events. This tidbit of information is not included in any disclosure. This is the kind of information you learn after you are a settled resident; but on closing day, after waiting for nine months or longer, you don't think about fire danger or disclosures. When closing day arrives the only thing on your mind is the last hurdle you must jump over-signing the paperwork. At this point you just eagerly glance over the papers looking for the signature line and sign your name. It is only after this ritual that you will get the keys to your new home and can finally begin to move all the boxes of stuff that you have spent the last several months packing. You may even have a truck already loaded up outside with movers waiting to get the all clear to begin unloading-she did. Her movers circled the block a few times then went for lunch while she signed papers and waited for a call from the title agent holding the pre-executed deed to confirm its recording. The disclosures aren't important. You sign them without even looking at them. They are between you and getting the keys, that's about it. You sign the papers and receive a copy that you take to your new home and tuck away in a drawer somewhere until something happens that triggers an interest in you to actually read them. It could be the news of a spreading wildfire in one of the nearby nature reserves or it could be an earthquake that shakes your house unexpectedly.

Earthquakes are always unexpected because there is no warning system in place; however if the Earthquake is a 'rolling quake' you may have some warning, albeit just a few seconds and that is probably not going to be long enough to do anything but consciously recognize the happening or steady some object close at hand. She recalls standing in her kitchen one early evening when she heard the garage doors rattling a few streets behind, then she heard the doors across the back street/alley just before she felt the townhouse shake while hearing her door rattle-that was a rolling quake. That quake wasn't enough to trigger a desire to see the disclosures, though she did look up a map on line to see the location of nearby fault lines. Knowing the location of major fault lines may provide some comfort, but after years of living in an area where quakes are a regular occurrence you learn that new fault lines are discovered periodically. If the epicenter of a quake occurs in a place not previously known as a fault line it is a new discovery and from that day forward the area may be prone to additional quakes.

Ironically, the first time she actually looked through the disclosures was when her house was under a short sale contract. She looked at them because she was sifting through the stack of paperwork from the home purchase, sorting it into throw away, keep, and give to the new homebuyer piles. Reading the disclosures gave her some solace as she thought, "Who wants to live in a high fire danger area anyway? Who wants to live in an area with fires, and mountain lions, and rattlers? Not I!"

In her subdivision the sources of wildlife fear were the rattlesnakes on the hiking trails and the coyotes that roamed freely throughout the night and sometimes brazenly in the light of day. She accepted that living in a new development adjacent to a natural wildlife habitat would come with the sounds and occasional sighting of the wildlife indigenous to the area. She was out jogging one early evening after nightfall, heading up one of only two village escape routes-an inclining side street that led past an elementary school and a skate park just beyond on the left. Just ahead of her several adult coyotes entered the street from the service road that intersected it. As soon as she spied the coyotes she slowed her jog to assure she did not intercept their path as they crossed the street. There was no time to consider what she should do if they changed their direction and moved toward her. She probably would have thrown out her arm with her hand pointing in the opposite direction and shouted, "Go Home!" like she had done in the past when being charged by a dog that had extended its owner's property line out into the street. It's not like she had anything to throw, except her house keys and cell phone. As it was, they crossed without incident then continued their run on the service road up toward the ridge. Although that was the closest she had ever been to coyotes, it was not the first time she encountered them. One late afternoon she saw a few on the local community college and public golf range. They were just walking around the edge of the range like kids shagging for balls. What a strange site!

Before she lived in California the only coyote she had ever heard of was the cartoon character and that one did not at all sound like the ones she heard late at night or early in the morning while they wandered the development. There is no mistaking their sound because the sounds coyotes make are eerie and unsettling. When they cry they sound like cats in heat or crying babies. When a whole pack starts up, they make yip and yelp sounds then howl like wolves. If you listen for the barks of resident dogs, you can track the coyote pack as it moves throughout the development. Encountering coyotes could be frightening but not nearly as scary as a mountain lion.

She recalls the picture she saw in the community newspaper of the mountain lion sunning herself on the ninth fairway of the golf course in a neighboring gated community. After reading that newspaper article, she had a few moments fear of being overrun by a mountain lion every time she jogged along the ridge. The fear usually started when she was at the most remote section of the jog. She would try to calculate how long it would take a mountain lion to overtake her if she was right, HERE, wherever that was along the jog route. She would imagine the lion starting out at some point beyond the ridge and as she jogged back and it got closer, she would wonder how fast she had to run to make her escape. There was one point along the route where she knew that in order to escape the imaginary mountain lion, now most certainly about to overtake her, she would have to climb an electric tower. There were electric towers placed periodically along the service road and one that sat at the very top of the ridge. The thought of climbing the tower was unnerving because along the bottom section metal stakes protruded outward from the frame in a 45° angle. She never really solved how she would avoid the metal stake issue. In her fantasy they were not there to deter her from escape if needed. At this point in her jog she would pick up her pace to a sprint and maintain that speed until she reached an imaginary point of safety.

Her night jogs never included the 'escape from a wild animal' thought game because she never jogged along the ridge at night. First, it was unlit, so would have been dangerous, even under the light of a full moon. There were too many ruts, dips and holes in the trail and it was not worth risking a twisted ankle or worse. She preferred jogging at night, even in the cooler days of winter because it was almost always a calming experience, though on a few rare occasions while on a night jog she ran through a light mist that caused a bubbling skin reaction on her face. It was likely some plant emission that caused several boil-like swellings on one of her cheeks. Whatever the source, the boils disappeared within fifteen minutes after she ingested an allergy pill.

Now as she jogs the only mist she feels is the fog, thick and cold. She glances up to see any sign of the moon but the fog is too thick and not even a hazy glow of its rise can be seen through the enveloping wetness. She looks ahead and sees that it has already swallowed the whole village. She slows to a walk because she can no longer see but a few feet in front of her. She is aware by the feel on the decline that she is nearing the bottom and is careful not to misjudge the end of sidewalk and trip off the curb. She can see a stop sign through the haze and uses that as a point of reference. She sees the headlight beams of a car approaching the intersection she is about to cross and moves backward to the brush lining the sidewalk until it passes. She quickly crosses the street and can see the village monument lit up for the night. The lights are now lit along the rear of the building and a few porch lights are on. She is glad to close the door on the fog and feel the inviting warmth inside.

While performing her bedtime routine a thought crosses her mind and it is not "will they come" for she knows without knowing that they will most certainly come on a night like this, a night with a thick fog under a full moon. Yes, they will come. They always come on a night like this. Yes, they will come and they will come for her as always. They always come for her on a night like this. Yes, they will most definitely come for her and she will go, as usual. Yes, they will come and she will go, but will she remember? Sometimes she remembers and she believes that sometimes they come and she goes but she does not remember. Will she remember this time? Will she want to remember? Can she choose to remember? Can she choose either way? If she does remember, what will she remember?

In the past, when they came and she went and remembered she was slightly changed. Something lingered within her, like a thought, an idea, a feeling, an understanding, a truth of some sort that was new to her but natural, comfortable, and at home within her. She felt the same way when she was first learning to play piano. There was a point in the earlier stages of the learning process when she realized she had the ability to play and could do so if she practiced. The practice began to take on a natural progression with a deeper meaning. She was no longer just following instructional steps, she was in control, directing her action, manipulating the play creatively.

Each time they came and she went and remembered linked to the time prior and also worked to propel her further beyond, like in practice. She felt an order, a progression to the process. A progression of knowledge and understanding of events that are predestined. Events predestined that include her and many others. This is perfectly natural to her and she does not know why. It is as natural as knowing they come in the fog. Tonight they will come in the fog. She knows they will come in the fog and they will come for her and she will go.

15

One last thought occurs to her as she turns out the light and of this she is also quite certain. They have come in the fog for her and she has gone ever since she was a small child.

Chapter Two
The Early Connection
α

Her childhood home was built in a tucked away suburban Pennsylvania neighborhood on land previously used as a grazing field, part of a working farm. At one time horses and cows graced the farm though she can only recall the cows. The cows were large, intimidating, and a little stinky. They were corralled behind an electric fence and the neighborhood children would tickle their noses with a long wheat weed if ever they were within reach. The farm owners were tolerant (they had children too) and generous with their corn harvest each year, towing a full cart to divide among the neighbors who had each hired contractors to build a home of their own design along the pebble and tarred street that dead-ended to a woods.

At the top of the street, named after the man who lived there, was a nice house that sat backwards, the front facing a wood that abutted a well traveled road below. The stately homes to the left and right of it were also backwards, with large front lawn areas meant to be backyards landscaped with fruit trees. The after school hang out took place in the house on the right, where mini-bike riding, music, ping-pong, pool, and Star Trek filled the hours before dinner. Her family physician lived in the house on the left and many years later, his daughter and her senator husband purchased the house in the middle. There were two homes, one old and one newly built along a gravel and mud lane that curved the backyards of the houses on the right side of her street. At the end of that lane, hidden behind a row of large spreading pines, sat one of the oldest homes original to the farm compound. If you walked (driving was not an option because it was almost always blocked by a chain link or a tree stump) beyond that home down the grass road forged with the large tires of a tractor, you would wind around to the right and partially through the west end of a small wood that opened to planting fields on the left, cows on the right, and eventually the end of the farm marked by a couple of older homes adjacent to an access road impassable after a heavy snow and otherwise full of deep ridges and dips, and filled with large quarry type rocks. Only people who lived there or those who were welcome would try to navigate that road.

If you turned right at the T shape intersection at top of her street you would decline along the lane abutting a public school grounds on the left and a section of land later developed with nice upper middle class homes on the right. The lane continues up a short incline where it merges into a triangular lot that abuts the locked Eastern gate of the school sitting just beyond the track and football field on one side and the main road curving up from below the three backward houses on the other. That triangular lot served as the school bus stop for several private and public schools in the area and the small gate house just inside the Eastern gate was the only refuge children had while waiting for the bus on a windy winter's morning.

The school grounds were a play magnet for all the neighborhood children. They watched football games during the school year and dance recitals held in the auditorium during summer vacation. They listened to the marching band practice on Saturday mornings in late summer and early in the evenings once the fall school session started. After a hard snow they jumped off a short wall at the Southeast lawn and onto the high pile of coal brought in each year to heat the building in winter. They road their bikes up and down the elongated loop surrounding the school and occasionally along the cinder track edging the football field. When she was on the

Intermediate School Track and Field Team she trained on the long, steep, tiered half-step set of stairs on the side of the school parallel to the lane. The large open pillared porch at the top of the stairs was a favorite hang out and where she and her best friend first applied the phrase, "If there's a will there's a way" when they figured out how to open a capped bottle without an opener. If she wasn't playing around the school or her friend's house she was likely somewhere in the woods at the bottom of her dead-end street.

She regularly disappeared for hours, walking along the winding paths, exploring small caverns, playing in large hollowed bushes-they made excellent houses-and from the top wood, swinging on thick vines attached to trees rooted along the hillside above the moving creek that weaved its way through the middle of the v-shaped bottom wood. She was always comfortable there and never felt alone, even in her solitude. Sometimes she had the company of other neighborhood children-it was their woods. One afternoon her best friend, two and half years her senior, was bloodied there. They were swinging on the vines-they called them 'Tarzan vines' because it was possible to swing and catch another close hanging vine and if you pushed off hard enough from a few of the main vines you could swing all the way out over the steep incline and the running creek below. A tight grip was essential; but when her friend took a turn on one of the vines she could not get a good grip. She slipped and fell into the middle of a thicket bush, emerging with a small stick protruding from her nose, a bleeding cut on her lip, several scrapes on her face, and a few arm and leg bruises. Lucky for her that she had not swung out over the cliff before falling-that would have been much worse. When someone got hurt in play that was bad but when you're a kid, the worst thing, the thing you think of when you know the injury is not fatal, is getting caught, so of course you try to avoid that if at all possible. They sneaked into her friends basement bathroom where they made a good attempt at trying to clean up the wounds while scheming how they could hide it from their mothers. No such luck! They were found out, suffered a talking to and in recounting the adventure her friend's new nickname, 'Butterfingers' was born.

She never suffered anything beyond a knee scraping in the woods, but did not escape childhood unscathed. She dove nose bridge first into the corner of a metal milk box earning her first set of several stitches and rode head first into a car bumper while sledding one winter near the northwesterly edge of the woods. She was lying on her stomach and moving quickly on a snow/ice pack toward a sled/ski path the neighborhood kids forged and was unable to hard steer the sled to avoid the parked truck. Instead of rolling off before impact she just froze and held on, not even ducking (which may have saved her from a worse injury) before slamming head first into the rear bumper. No blood (thanks to the headscarf she wore), just a bad headache, a bump, and humility-how stupid to not roll off, right? She was pretty brave after that-figured she had to show the others so she pushed herself to try anything that the older kids were doing and rarely doubled a "dog dare ya" challenge. There were plenty of opportunities to show bravery too, especially while they were building the new houses on the track of land just east of her street.

She was old enough to climb ladders and walk across the wooden planks that crossed the deep trenches dug along the foundation of the homes being built. The neighborhood children would explore the houses on the weekends, mostly on Sunday afternoons when there was no chance of finding any workers there. Sometimes the owners would come to see their house in progress and if they were in the house they would hide until they left. On one such occasion they climbed up into the attic of a house and peered at the couple visiting through the fan vent. They were sure they would be found out and held their breath trying hard not to make a sound. This was especially difficult for her because she always found humor in those moments. She wanted to laugh but if she started there was nothing short of death that could have stopped her.

Those newly built houses replaced an apple orchard spotted with the trees she learned to climb on. The orchard had one resident. She was a mysterious woman living in a small wooden house, not more than a shack really, that sat at the Northwest corner of the field not far from the lane. She was mysterious because she was rarely seen, but "us guys" as the neighborhood kids called themselves knew there was a woman living there. They also knew that something happened in that small house, something bad, really bad.

She knew it was really bad because her parents would not speak of it and all the other parents in her neighborhood would not talk about it either, at least not openly. She knew something 'was up' because one day the shack was there and the next it was half burned down and within a week bulldozed flat, all the wood piled and moved off the property to who knows where.

Of course nothing like that happens without the birth of an urban legend. In this case the legend was of a lady dressed in white who wandered the bottom wood and neighboring farmland. If there was any kid who had not claimed to have seen her he or she would at least admit they heard her wailing as she supposedly moved in the wood searching for something. There were some modifications to the legend once the neighborhood kids learned about a man who lived somewhere near the bottom wood at the Southwesterly section of the farm. He supposedly had a salt pellet rifle and the boys in the neighborhood swore he chased after them threatening to shoot if he got close enough. So they modified the legend of the woman in white to include this strange man-he shot his wife (the lady in white) who returned to wander the woods looking for him and to take her revenge.

The kids did not know what actually became of the lady who lived in that shack. It is possible (likely) that she moved into one of the other houses on the farm or maybe she died. When you're a kid though, logical inferences can't compete with the strong imaginings that are a part of childhood. For her, the lady in the shack was not the most mysterious thing about the orchard. The most mysterious thing was that her first flying dream took place there.

One summer when she was no older than nine she found herself in a lucid dream. She was fully aware she was dreaming as she flew high, circling above the orchard under the light of a full moon. She felt the cool night air against her cheeks as it gently brushed her hair back while she rose up higher and higher until the apple trees looked miniature below. She could see over the whole neighborhood, the farm, and out further to the Western hills. It was fantastic! She was able to control her height, speed, and direction with ease. It was so natural, so real, so much fun! When she awoke in her bed later that night she was excited for having had such a thrilling dream of flying, flying! She didn't realize it then, but that was probably the first hint of an epiphany she would have about what she has come to appreciate as one of her two connections to nature-birds.

It is not unusual to feel a connection with birds-many people do. She met a businesswoman who named her company after her favorite bird, numerous other people who were avid bird watchers, others who put out bird baths and feeders on their property, and a friend who shared several experiences she had with birds she believed carried messages to her at various times in her life. The messages were akin to warnings and each came to fruition in later events. Wow, right? Remember that old saying, "A little birdie told me?" Listen, always listen closely to the birds if and when they speak to you.

She was too young to understand or appreciate her flying dream. It just was, like every other aspect of childhood. The underlying meaning of such things only came with deeper probing, the likes of which one can only acquire after heady consideration, right? There is a widely accepted notion that children, like animals can feel and see things that adults, after years of programming to accept mostly limited mainstream concepts as truths, are blind to. If an adult experiences something extraordinary it is usually dismissed as some anomaly. It was caused by something he ate, or she was overly tired, and so on. Is it possible to maintain the sensitivity of a child, to nurture and develop it while growing into adulthood? For her, seeing there were connections to her perceptions of the world around her through her interaction with nature was paramount because it provided a point of reference. She had revelations about her place in relation to nature that came in regular pace throughout her childhood and into her adult years. Considered as a whole these moments of clarity were quite remarkable and perhaps profound; however if considered individually they seemed simply ordinary, like understanding a concept in geometry or learning the harmony to a new song in church choir.

Her second connection to nature were trees. In her youth she would lie flat on her back on her friend's front lawn in the wee hours of an Indian summer morning looking up at a row of deeply rooted Pines standing tall across the tar and pebbled lane running in front the property. In that setting she would feel the life within the branches swaying softly in the light breeze. It was more than just the realization that the trees were alive-everyone knows that! It was something more, something like communication. She sensed emotion and understood without thinking that the trees, these trees, were one, with us, and in that moment she felt euphoric. She felt something else too. She felt protected. She felt a natural alliance but had no idea what it meant or how powerful it would become. Trees provided a platform, a safe haven to climb and perch. There is an art to climbing and descending a tree, like a ballet of balance and strength. The climb is not the difficult part. Anyone who has been high up in a tree understands this because when you climb you naturally climb with the convenience of branch placement near your grasp and this rarely takes you in a straight line upward. While climbing you maneuver to the right and left reaching for the perfect branch to hold your weight, testing it as you pull up. When its time to descend there is a disadvantage because you are testing new branches with the entire weight of your body. One wrong move could bring you tumbling quickly to the bottom. This is where courage and a leap of faith come in.

She spent a lot of time climbing trees around the neighborhood but not the one she saw them in. The tree they were perched in had branches that were not thick enough to hold her weight and were much too straight to climb. She was no more than eight when she stood on that warm summer night looking out her bedroom window that overlooked her front yard still wet from a day of stormy weather with lightning striking so close you could smell sulphur. At first she saw one, then two of them in a tree across the street that stood next to the wooden pole housing the street light, and serving as anchor to the sloping telephone and electrical line wires that crossed over to her house.

So strange to see but it was almost like watching some kind of real time cartoon because they wore no clothing yet their bodies were not anatomic. They looked a little like Astronauts because their heads appeared almost helmet like, large and grey-white in color. What may seem incredulous is that she was not at all frightened or even surprised at the sight.

24

In fact, it seemed expected somehow. She knew without knowing that she was supposed to be at the window at that precise moment to see them. She also knew one more thing. They were there for her.

She stared at them and she could feel their returned stare. She waited but nothing happened except she became overwhelmed with fatigue and felt her eyes grow heavy. She returned to her bed for just for a minute to rest her eyes but could not stay awake any longer.

Chapter Three
Awakening Senses

Ω

The decade before she became a teenager was filled with international political unrest, contradiction, and murder. There was the sudden death of film legend and sex icon Marilyn Monroe on August 5, 1962, followed by the thirteen days of confrontation in October-the Cuban Missile Crisis. The high moaning of air raid siren drills pierced the air regularly and children were taught to run home to make shift bomb shelters or if in school, drop under their desks whenever they sounded.

Time stood still for the nation when the 35th President of the United States, John Fitzgerald Kennedy was assassinated and if asked years later anyone old enough to remember could recall exactly where they were on November 22, 1963, at 12:30 pm central time.

When the Beatles debuted in America on the Ed Sullivan Show that aired February 9, 1964, they provided America's youth and a large adult population with a much needed distraction. The songs they wrote were simple, with catchy lyrics, a beat you could dance to and in the early years especially, expressed themes of falling in love. 'Beatlemania' swept the nation, welcoming everyone to embark on six years of their magical tour of music playing in the background while the nation was shocked by the loss of two more dynamic leaders. Martin Luther King, Jr., who led the civil rights movement from the mid 1950s until he was assassinated in April 1968, followed just two months later by the killing of President Kennedy's brother, Attorney General Robert Kennedy in June of 1968.

The blood continued to flow in the following summer with the brutally horrific Tate and LaBianca murders by the Manson family on August 9, 1969. The senseless nature of these crimes was a wake up call to the American people in part because they were committed by young people who appeared perfectly normal, like the girl or guy next door, except their leader Manson, who put on a crazed and evil face whenever photographed.

Less than a week later, on August 16, 1969, the three day music and art fair 'Woodstock' began, billed as an Aquarian Exposition: 3 Days of Peace & Music. There were an estimated 300,000 young people in attendance at that White Lake New York dairy farm and a reported two deaths-one heroin overdose and one young man run over by a tractor as he lay asleep inside a sleeping bag.

Amid all this there was The Vietnam War. The war was a struggle between nationalists who wanted a unified communist government and the United States and the South Vietnamese who wanted to stop the spread of communism. The United States' involvement in the Vietnam War was protested by many, but stories of the protests were weaved into the updates about the war as propaganda and were mostly focused on teenage and young adult rebellion, labeled as the love and peace movement. Hippies led the war protesters and draft dodgers, groups of 'flower children' and others led marches, set up communes, and rallied on college campuses across the country. As the anti-war movement grew stronger, the radio networks aired tunes that told simple stories of peace, love and awakening. Artists like Joan Baez, Judy Collins, Joni Mitchell, James Taylor, Graham Nash, David Crosby, Neil Young, Stephen Stills, and so many others captured the hearts of more than one generation. She heard the same question repeated in song lyrics, on talk-radio, in school, and in conversations everywhere as if it was a common theme to a play they were all forced to sit through, "Why are we in this war?" Americans were getting fed up with the lack of information and the lack of progress made in the war effort. People grew suspicious about reports of war casualties and began to press for answers about the missing in action. Then a tragedy occurred on the homeland that captured everyone's attention and shook the senses of anyone who believed that college campuses were safe from violence. When the news stations reported the Kent State campus shootings of four student protesters attending a rally on May 4, 1970, shockwaves of disbelief reeled throughout the country. The students were shot by troops who were otherwise engaged to protect the American public. The Kent State shootings worked to dismantle the trust Americans had in government leadership and further emphasized the need to reunite the country. She was thirteen years old, listening to the musical messages flowing from the radio and the song of the day was "Ohio" by Crosby, Stills, Nash, & Young: *"Tin soldiers and Nixon coming. We're finally on our own. This summer I hear the drumming-Four dead in Ohio."*

She did not fully grasp the events of the 60's until well into the next decade. Although she remembers every horrific happening she was still a child, sheltered and at a distance. There were local school race riots but not in the parochial school she attended. The events played in the background of her young life without great meaning because they were not personal to her. She had a child's sense of curiosity for the macabre details because she had never been exposed to anything like it before-like a train wreck, so tragic yet you can't look away. She was on the cusp of womanhood and uncertain how to handle the emotional roller coaster she found herself riding without an end in sight. She turned to music in her struggle to understand how she would fit into the world that was opening up all around her. There were questions and answers in the song lyrics and the music captured her deeply.

28

She related to the messages she heard and she worked hard to understand the meaning behind them. She wanted to fully feel the songs. She attempted to learn how to play an acoustic guitar and although she did not put in the time necessary to master it, she began to write poetry and song lyrics and she continued to sing. She sang every chance she had, much to the chagrin of those within ear. From the time she was a child she felt the desire to sing whether it was in the back seat of the family car or alone in her room. It was a refuge and a way she could express her feelings without openly speaking them. She would learn all the lyrics of every song she heard then sing along with the radio and to the records she would spin on her 45 and LP turntable. Music and song provided the platform and outlet she needed to express her moody and restless state at the start of her teenage years.

Being a teenager in the early 70's had some advantages, especially if you had older siblings. Older siblings on the brink of adulthood forge a path of trials and tribulations unlike any before and the steps and falls they take along the way help to build a sort of foundation or template of do's and don'ts parents refer to (if only subconsciously) when parenting the children that follow. The first child has the most pictures taken and is given the most attention, naturally, because they are the first. By the time child number three or four comes along most parents are over it. She heard of a boy who's parents showed pictures of an older sibling saying it was him when the truth was that they just stopped taking pictures of him at one point. They were over it. She was a middle child and by the time she reached her teenage years her parents were rather numb to the whole experience, so she mostly flew well under their radar.

Beginning her freshman year she went to public high school and expressed her newfound freedom by engaging in activities like smoking and drinking, skipping classes, thumbing for rides (her father once drove by while she was engaged in this activity but never mentioned a word of it) and hanging out with friends who put together local garage bands. She attended school dances but rarely danced because the boys all stood at the stage watching the band while the girls hung around in back talking about how stupid the boys looked-like groupies-Ha! Once she and a classmate decided they would swap boyfriends during a dance and their boyfriends just went along with it dumbly. That was as wild as it got and it only lasted one year. In her sophomore year she entered the college scene by way of her best friend-remember Butterfingers? It was then that she had her first real grownup relationship.

Butterfingers attended college in state and she would visit on weekends regularly. They engaged with groups of students in endless hours of conversation that spanned topics on current events, study subjects, and anything enlightening (those topics usually entered the circle in the late evening hours) that held the group's interest. It was an informal exchange of ideas but if you really felt strongly about something you had to be well prepared for debate. It was on one such occasion that she met the guy who would be her first real love.

He was the roommate of the guy Butterfingers was dating and he happened to reside close enough to her hometown that made it possible to continue the relationship whenever he visited his family during the school year. He was the perfect boyfriend from her father's prospective because he appeared responsible-this one actually came to the front door and would sit and chat it up with him while waiting to take her out on a date. If her father knew what went on during the weekends at college he may have had a different attitude but if he was comparing him to some of her earlier boyfriends she was sure he saw him as a definite improvement. This guy even brought him gifts from his authentic Italian household, like homemade wine and pepperoni cured in his attic. She fell for him hard and fast. He was extremely handsome-Butterfingers' mother said he had "bedroom eyes" and she was right about that. His eyes were amazing, large, dark and always smiling. Butterfingers teased her that his mother was likely standing outside his bedroom door when she stayed over, whispering, "Bambinos, bambinos." Ha! If this was true it would not have bothered her in the least. She adored his sweet mother who was a gem of a woman that treated her like one of the family from the first day they met. She raised her son to be his own man and he was. He was well spoken, had a passion for politics (she attended a political convention but not her senior prom) and he seemed to adore her, even during those tough post puberty years when she was teasingly described by her father as having an hour glass figure with all the sand at the bottom. In spite of his shoulder-length hair and the age difference, her parents welcomed the relationship and it lasted until she departed for college.

She prepared for college while still in high school, reading material beyond the normal school requirements. In high school the trend among students was to read only as much as necessary for passing tests, so discussions around books was mostly limited to filling in a classmate who had clearly not taken the time to read assignments. Teachers started giving tests on material you could not know unless you had read the entire text. They were wise to Cliff Notes-remember those? So they geared the classroom discussions away from the reading material to force students to pick up the book and actually read it. She had no issue with reading, regularly immersing herself in anything she could pull from the library that promised to be interesting. One read in particular started her on a life-changing journey.

Her view of the world's reality began to slowly change while she read what was then referred to in her extended circle of friends as the Carlos Casteneda trilogy, though the number

31

of books in the series were more than three. The first three Don Juan books, *'The Teachings of Don Juan: A Yaqui Way of Knowledge,' 'Separate Reality: Further Conversations with Don Juan,' and "Journey to Ixtian: The Lessons of Don Juan"* had a profound effect upon her, probably because they were so strange and she had reached a point in her life where she wanted to understand everything on a deeper level.

She wanted to experience life as she never had before and there was so much that she had never done. She and Butterfingers attended psychotherapy sessions at the free clinic because it was 'hip' to do so. They hung out with friends who explored their musical talent on acoustic guitars and they attended poetry readings and jam sessions in the coffee houses located near a city college campus. She began to look at the world around her differently, focusing on the detail rather than the bigger picture.

She allowed herself the pleasure of contemplation, feeling the moment in full awareness-she began to meditate. During meditation she sometimes listened to nature tracks, like ocean waves or whale sounds. She practiced breathing techniques that included using her diaphragm to push her stomach outward as she breathed inward instead of merely inflating her lungs. She chanted 'Ohms' by breathing in deeply and humming, "ooohhhmmm" as she exhaled. Om (or Aum) is a mantra and according to Wikipedia, the mystical Sanskrit sound of Hindu origin, sacred and important in various Dharmic religions such as Hinduism, Buddhism, and Jainism. The practice cleared her head of the usual clutter, the noise distractions that continuously interrupt one's train of thought. Meditation provided a path to a conscious stream of unexpected warmth, like when you swim in cold water and cross through a warm current. It provided a sense of calm and well-being.

As she gained more experience with meditation she began to feel additional benefits. One was that she felt that she had a heightened understanding of the world around her, as if her inner instinct switch slipped into a higher gear. It was in this state that, on the morning after her high school graduation and bonfire party at the wooded edge of the farm planting fields that followed, she departed for the state's main college campus to register for summer term classes

Chapter Four
Understanding Meditation

≋

At college she continued her swim in the sea of meditation and broadened her prospective on meditative teachings. She read Zen series books like *Zen and the Art of Archery*-a classmate left that one in her mailbox. She participated in lively discussions about the self, and purpose of existence. Picasso said that the meaning of life is to find your gift and the purpose of life is to give it away. She saw Meditation as a path leading to a quiet mind where one can envision a mission or quest upon which to focus then practice as a means to uncover hidden talents, exposing their gift.

She learned that meditation is therapeutic and when used for healing purposes, a great aid in reducing the stress that accompanies illness and sometimes blocks the healing process by prohibiting the body's natural immune system from working at its full potential.

Practicing meditation can also re-wire and fire the neurons in the brain and there is scientific research backing this up. Neuroplasticity is the brain's ability to reorganize itself by forming new neural connections. Paul Tingen in his article titled, *"Using Mindfulness to Rewire the Brain"* writes that until the 1980s it was believed that the brain developed in childhood until it reached a finished form then stayed pretty much the same throughout adulthood. So our "consciousness was seen as nothing more than the byproduct of the cellular pathways" in the brain along which neurons transmit electrical signals. The interactions of these neurons carry our thoughts, memories, and emotions and supposedly remain fixed, as written by Nicholas Carr in his book, *The Shallows: What the In-*

ternet Is Doing to Our Brains. In the 1980s Professor Michael Merzenich conducted research that resulted in the accepted view that the brain constantly rewires itself in response to changes in our feelings, thoughts, experiences, and the way we use our body.

Today, neuroscience is governed by what is referred to as Hebb's rule: "Cells that fire together wire together." So to practically apply the rule one must feel a sense of well-being in order to achieve a sense of well-being. How can this be done? Science of The Buddha may hold the key.

The essence of Buddhist teaching is to use mindfulness to obtain a singularity of thought that does not trigger a worn neuron pathway of unhappiness and suffering. Happiness can only be achieved though happiness. So one must allow a happy thought to wear the neuron pathway and trigger more happy thoughts. Tingen provides an example of using the mantra "This is a happy moment" to achieve this.

Another more intricate example of using a meditation exercise to re-wire the brain's neurons was aired on the Dr. Oz television program and introduced by Deepak Chopra when he appeared as a guest and spoke about transcendental meditation. Chopra went through a simple meditation step by step process and challenged the television audience to try it daily for 21 days with a promise of stress relief.

Here is a slight variation of this meditation (other similar meditations can be found on Chopra's web site, choprateachers.com). Step 1-contemplate gratitude. What is gratitude but a thankfulness for all the positive things in our lives, right? So we think about what we appreciate about our life, both big and small, including past and current events, and future opportunities. After we contemplate gratitude for several minutes, we continue on to Step 2, asking ourselves these questions, reflecting on each one for several minutes before going on to the next: 1)Who am I? 2)What is my purpose?

3)What do I want? 4)What makes me happy? Step 3, sense your body and specifically, your heart.

This meditation reminds her of when she attended a personal growth retreat session where the Productive Learning and Leisure instructor led a group of approximately 100 coworkers on a meditative journey. They were all asked to close their eyes and envision a wooded area with a path that they were walking along. The instructor provided visual clues of what they may encounter along the path and after several minutes it was not at a difficult to be there, along that path and experiencing the wood with stunning clarity. They experienced sensual clues like the feel of the sun's warmth filtering through openings in tree branches above and the feel of a soft breeze against their cheek. There were also audio clues, like the sound of a rambling brook in the not so far off distance and that of a bird fluttering by. She heard the sound of moving water, pleasant and steady. She heard the sound of the movement of a bird's wings through the air. This wood was very real and much like the wood near her childhood home. The walk along the path in the wood was familiar to her and extremely pleasant. She felt happiness in that moment and did not want it to end.

The journey continued until they came to a fork in the path where they were faced with a choice. They could take the path forward and into the entrance of a cave or take the path that veered off to the right and headed around the cave. If the choice was made to veer around the cave there was a resting spot where they could stop and enjoy the scenery while waiting for the group to complete their exploration of the cave. If anyone chose not to enter the cave it was not shared. It seemed to her that everyone would choose the cave-why not, right? Why would you want to wait on the sidelines and miss the experience of an unexplored cave? She chose the cave without hesitation and imagined the entrance getting larger as she got closer though she still could not see what was inside. Their mediation lead navigated them through the entrance and described at once the change in temperature. Unlike the warm path the cave was much cooler and slightly damp but not at all unpleasant. The cave lighting was bright enough as not to totally hinder their line of sight as they slowly moved forward but not so bright as to allow them to see any further ahead than the point described by their guide. They reached a section of the cave that was lit more intensely with a warm glow that radiated from the cave walls and beckoned them forward and into a room with a temperature as warm as the sunlit path outside. There was a figure sitting in the light, back against the cave wall. The group was instructed to take a seat on the floor in front of and facing the figure. The guide told them that they sat facing that one person, who, if given the chance, they could see and converse with, right there and then. The person could be anyone, even someone they never met, a famous politician for example or a celebrity. This was the one person they most wanted to see and talk with at that point in their lives. They were told to envision this person sitting before them.

She saw her father. He was smiling warmly and his brown eyes held a sparkle that showed her how happy he was to see her. Nearly ten years earlier he had been diagnosed with a prostate issue, had surgery, then was told he was 'cured'. The family was hopeful and because he was not one to complain, she didn't even see the prostate issue as serious. The fatal error was the lack of proper follow up-no blood work was ordered. A proper follow up would have revealed that there was a deeper, more serious problem; however even if known it may not have had any positive or long-term effect on the end result because her father had already decided he would not participate in chemotherapy. Even if he had, there was no guarantee that taking the option would have provided him with the extended quality of life that would have been worth all the pain and suffering chemotherapy patients go through.

During a conversation they had about the possibility of world destruction by atomic bombs her father told her that if it ever happened he hoped he would be struck right on the head. He did not have any desire to live in a world that was only partially like the one he was accustomed to. So she understood why he would choose not to exchange his quality of life for the possibility of a slightly extended lifetime. If it was his time he was ready to go.

He died of a fast-moving and brutally fatal bone cancer and she did not see him to say goodbye before he past. She was totally wrapped up in work, grad school, and caring for her daughter and had not fully understood the gravity of his situation. She was in denial and because the illness took hold and moved so quickly, not at all prepared to lose him after three short months. The Christmas Holiday visit she planned was too late-he past away on 1 November.

In the cave she sat facing her Dad and apologized for not being there for him at the end. He told her to move forward and said, "Call your mother." She flashed back to when she was at the funeral home kneeling in front of the rented casket (he was cremated). She was looking at his gaunt face for the last time, trying to recognize him, to find the face she knew there. He had lost so much weight that she could not place this last face with any she had at any point in her memory, not even the pictures she had seen of him when he was a thin young man. Then she noticed the scar on his cheek from the Korean War shrapnel that grazed his face and tore off two of his knuckles-He was awarded a purple heart for that sacrifice. Her gaze went to the knuckles and she heard his voice in her head, "Take my hand" and while she reached down to touch his hand she thought she saw it move slightly as if to raise up to meet hers.

Back in the cave there were some tears, some joy, and for her, some sense of closure. It was precisely what she needed to release the self-loathing and regret she held onto after the normal grieving process following her father's death ended. Meditative techniques like this one proved for her to be both therapeutic and enlightening. In terms of personal growth, in the two years she was fortunate enough to be part of a group that regularly learned and shared in these types of experiences she found a wealth of knowledge and self-awareness. She felt that she was getting closer to her core, the essence of her and closer to discovering (or rediscovering) her gift, what it would mean to her, and how it would work to shape her life moving forward. What she rediscovered ironically, were teachings and methods she was learning about and beginning to practice in her first year of college.

She had had no set expectation for any particular result from meditation and therefore was always pleasantly surprised by a positive post meditative experience. She found that the more regularly she practiced meditation, the more frequently she experienced euphoria in otherwise ordinary circumstances. Instantaneous gratitude for things most people overlook every day. The fantastically delicious first sip of coffee in the morning, the pleasure of looking at a beautiful landscape or walking with your head looking upward at a starry night. Simple pleasures, magnified. Meditation slowed her down enough so she could really "see" the world around her. She had a renewed appreciation and her enthusiasm for life reached a higher level, like when you feel you can accomplish anything because you have not yet learned that you can't or when a stimulating conversation turns on a switch inside that motivates you to explore a new path or revisit one you had abandoned. She was ever thirsty for more knowledge and struggled for the insight she hoped would help her come to terms with her inability to find a logical explanation for the strange happenings she continued to experience.

Chapter Five
The Third Eye

✪

Ever hear of the 'third eye'? There is a scientific basis for the belief that a small gland called the pineal gland (its name derived from the root of the word "pinea" which is Latin for "pinecone") is a third eye. This gland, located in the brain's exact geometric center, is the size of a pea and secretes the hormone melatonin, which regulates our sleep cycles.

In Steven Bancarzl's article, *"Silva Mind Control"* he writes that, "[t]he pineal gland is also thought to secrete a chemical known as DMT, which has the nickname of 'The Spirit Molecule'. Some believe that DMT (a chemical compound that has a powerful hallucinogenic effect when digested) is released during dreaming, spiritual and mystical experiences, and at the time of death." How does this gland resemble the human eye?

According to Dr. David Klein, Science Daily, "The photoreceptors of the retina strongly resemble the cells of the pineal gland." The pineal gland has vitreous fluid like an eye and according to a study published in Experimental Eye Research, light sensing proteins like those in the retina, raising "the possibility that direct photic events may occur in the mammalian pineal gland." The calcite micro crystals inside the pineal gland produce a bioluminescence-cold light ranging in the blue-green light spectrum, similar to the transparent light seen in underwater sea creatures. Potentially the gland could be developed for tissue transparency application and a more precise abnormal cell detection than is available through thermal imaging.

Dr. Cheryl Craft, Ph.D., Chair of the Department of Cell and Neurobiology, University of Southern California writes: "Under the skin in the skull of a lizard lies a light-responsive 'third eye' which is the evolutionary equivalent of the bone-encased, hormone-secreting pineal gland in the human brain. The human pineal is denied access to light directly, but like the lizard's "third eye," it shows enhanced release of its hormone, melatonin, during the night. The pineal gland is the 'mind's eye.' Dissected, the reptile's pineal looks much like an eye, with the same shape and tissue." Although there is no definitive proof that the pineal gland can 'see' beyond the third dimension, there is biological proof that it has the potential to function as an actual eye.

Equally incredible, scientists have found that the pinealocytes-the main cells in the pineal gland-are similar to piezoelectric crystals found within the inner ear. Piezoelectric crystals are used to pick up sound vibrations from electromagnetic radiation, and are used in things like microphones, radios, and mobile communication type devices. The calcite micro-crystals in the pineal gland are similarly responsive to electromagnetic energy outside the body and can also produce its own electromagnetic energy. If the pineal gland is picking up mobile communication frequencies what type of affect does this have? In her article, *The Peizolectric Effect and the Pineal Gland in the Human Brain* Debbie Edwards explains: "What this means is that any energies that produce electromagnetic response in relation to the Pineal gland could alter energy patterns within the body and brain from the central nervous system to sexual function . . . "

Research has shown that lower infrared band frequency waves can have negative affects on the mood and health of the human body whereas higher frequency waves can have positive affects. This may be why people living close to electrical power transmission towers have reported negative health affects and why there are concerns about holding cellular phones against the ear.

Other research on the third eye reveals that for many the pineal gland is calcified and this has a negative effect upon the gland's ability to produce melatonin and therefore negatively affects the sleep cycle. This is caused in part by the additives and preservatives in the foods we eat but mostly by our exposure to fluoride and heavy metals like aluminum. The fluoride found in toothpaste and even our drinking water will deposit in the pineal gland and work to calcify it. To avoid calcification of the pineal gland steer clear of fluoride, bromide, excessive amounts of calcium, mercury, and aluminum (this list is not exhaustive). Most of us have been exposed to these and other toxicities in our foods and personal care products, so where does that leave us if we just avoid exposure in the future? Research shows that it is possible to change the state of calcification of the pineal gland.

If you want to prevent calcification of your Pineal gland you can begin by eating foods that may work to decalcify the gland, like those rich in vitamin C and high in alkaline. Eat lemons, ginger, and raw apple cider vinegar. Try raw cocoa. Cocoa mixes well with plain yogurt and the result is really quite good. Eat organically grown fruits and vegetables. This can be pricey so you have to choose where you can reasonably avoid the toxins. Iodine and magnesium are also believed to decalcify the pineal gland. Basically, we should all read the ingredient labels before we purchase and ingest or use products and avoid an abundance of toxins. You can find all natural toothpaste, deodorant without aluminum, and if your tap water contains fluoride, either filter it properly or buy bottled water.

Want to explore opening your third eye? There is a step by step instruction for the first and second awakening on the web site consiouslifenews.com. It is best to read up on the possible side affects before making a decision to move forward. According the information available, you may suffer headaches through the process and the process, once complete, is thought to be irreversible. Here is a small excerpt from the article on how to achieve the first awakening and second awakening. To begin, you chant the same mantra in an alto range five times in a row for three days in 24 hour intervals:

"The mantra to be used is 'Thoh,' pronounced 'TOE.'

1. Sit with your back straight. 2. Breathe in through your nose and hold your breath as long as is

comfortable. Place the tip of your tongue between the space of your slightly parted teeth. 3. Put a very light pressure onto the tongue with your teeth. Once your tongue is in position, release your breath slowly through your mouth, saying T-H-H-O-H-H in one long exhale."

The meditative mantras she chanted alone and with her friends were more similar to the one associated with the second awakening of the pineal gland. The second awakening should be attempted at least 10 days after the first awakening and is repeated once a week. It begins with a deep breathing exercise designed to relax and to focus. The mantra this time is the word 'May' slowly sounded out and like the first awakening and is repeated five times in an alto tone while concentration is focused on the penal gland, middle of the brain, and top of the head, at the crown chakra.

She followed the instruction for the first awakening and although she did not follow the exact timing for the 24 hour intervals, she did experience a strange sensation afterward. She had no headache but she did feel and hear a popping sensation, like when your ears pop while descending in an aircraft, only the popping was not in her ears. Immediately afterward it felt similar to a neck alignment that results in an instant muscle relaxation, but the area relaxed was near her eyebrows. It brings to mind an experience she had when she felt something deep inside her skull. She had moved from a moderate climate to one that was extremely hot and dry, the temperature rising to well over 100 in the shade-it literally felt like an oven outdoors. She had been indoors in a comfortable air-conditioned office and went outside to a temperature more than thirty degrees hotter. She stubbornly decided she could jog in that heat, remembering that in the past she jogged at high noon in the summer months. It was not a good idea. At the end of the jog, she was overheated, lightheaded and probably somewhat dehydrated. Once back at her apartment she attempted to cool down by drinking water but it was not working fast enough. She continued to feel strained and lightheaded. Then she suddenly felt a cooling of her head on the inside that followed a muffled swooshing sound, like that made by a tire inflator hand pump. It felt as though a light cool mist was sprayed onto her brain. She reasoned the cause was the opening of sweat glands on her scalp and the release of water onto her head. She never experienced it again, nor did she repeat jogging in excessive heat.

After completing the second awakening instructions she began to become more conscious of her peripheral vision, though her ability to focus there was really nothing new to her. She just had not practiced it on a regular basis. She found that especially in the early morning hours, just as the light of dawn made it possible to see some detail in the trees outside her window, she could look through the slats in blinds, shift her vision, then see an extension of the blinds, like they moved outward into a new three-dimensional state. Logic told her this was a mere optical illusion, but sometimes, if she maintained the focus, she could see detail outside that of the window blind edges. As strange as it seemed, she was looking at a space that seemed to extend beyond the widow blinds but at the same time located somewhere in between. On one occasion while

45

staring at the extended section of blinds she saw two enormous ape-like creature on all fours facing inward at the very top left edge of the blind extension. She explained this away as black spots that appear sometimes with eye strain. Whatever it was, it freaked her out to the extent that she made no further attempt to recreate the optical illusion.

After her third eye awakening exercise she had a greater sense of awareness, both auditory and visual. She felt a stronger sense of purpose and desire to explore creativity. She found a new joy in fun and play and sought out the company of others who were creative and spontaneous.

Chapter Six
Spontaneity

In her first year of college she believed that spontaneity was the key to experiencing a memorable adventure. She made fast friends during this time and experienced a few 'firsts', like sneaking into the fenced pool area in the wee hours of the morning to skinny-dip with her summer lover and friend. What qualified this as a 'first' was the locked location, not the activity. She had her first skinny dip a year prior while visiting Butterfingers at the Jersey Shore.

Butterfingers and another local friend were working at the shore during summer break and she was stuck back in Pennsylvania, land-locked and lonely for her friends. It was the summer before her senior high school year and she had nothing remotely exciting on the agenda. She decided that she simply had to get in on some of that Jersey shore fun. So she took a bus into the city, walked to the Greyhound station and boarded another heading east and to the shore. She was so quick with the decision that she had not thought of making arrangements with her friends beforehand. It just had not occurred to her to plan the visit or that she might need a destination address. She just acted on impulse and after an uneventful ride on the Pennsylvania Turnpike, found herself in the middle of a lazy beachside town. She looked around seeing nothing about it that would give rise to its name and thought that it was likely named after driftwood and not for unruly resident or visitor behavior. She had no plan for the night but she knew it was too late to call anyone until morning, so she headed toward the shore, suitcase in hand, and looked for a spot where she could sit the night out.

Once at the beach she found a bench and planted herself at one end then proceeded to eat the last of a snack she bought during the one and only rest stop the bus driver made, permitting the travelers enough time to use the facilities, check out the vending machines and stretch their legs. While she chewed the second of two chocolate on chocolate cupcakes with cream filling and sipped cream soda through a straw a young long haired but clean shaven guy who looked like he was in his early twenties sat down next to her and started chatting her up.

He was a musician-played percussion in a band working the local clubs for the summer and had recently finished the last set for the night. She was immediately interested in learning everything she could from this cute guy who was from upstate New York. As he filled her in on what led him to the shore that summer she realized that even in the dim light she could see that his eyes were brilliantly blue. He had an easy way about him and though she tried to concentrate on his words her thoughts drifted as she scanned his face-the strong cut of his jawline and the one dimple that showed whenever he smiled-she was instantly attracted. Their conversation flowed like the rippling water off shore and the next several hours past quickly. He offered to stay with her until daylight then help her find the summer rental where Butterfingers was staying. Although she was not afraid to be alone she was nonetheless grateful for the company and at that moment could not imagine a better way to spend her first night in Wildwood.

At some point in the wee hours of the morning, they found themselves stripping off their clothes and walking toward the ocean. It was deliciously fun and quite refreshing to venture out into the cool water. The Atlantic tide was at the turning point and waves were gently caressing their naked bodies as they swam together. She was acutely aware of his lean taut body swimming so close to hers and she found herself aroused when they touched periodically. After a few minutes she tried to touch bottom but found they were too far off shore to do that and she instinctively reached for him. Not long after the kiss, the first, long, deep, sensual and salty kiss, she experienced the second 'first' of her life-they christened the Atlantic.

Back in 'Happy Valley' on that summer night in the closed and locked outdoor pool, the water was warm and inviting in contrast to the cool night air. She was floating on her back, enjoying the moment and inwardly smiling at their triumph in gaining access to the pool.

When the night security patrol car approached they went under water, holding their breath until the car's sharply piercing headlight beams moved on. That was not easy to do when you have an irresistible impulse to laugh. She was never very good at holding her breath-it was too unnatural. She was able to last just long enough to avoid discovery and although they continued their swim, the arrival of the night patrol broke the magical spell of their delinquent adventure and soon the chill of the night air overburdened the skinny-dip fun.

Her summer lover was also her very best friend. He was a good-looking, dark haired, darker eyed, creative, Italian, would-be furniture designer from Philadelphia. He was thoughtful, artistic, creative, fun, and like her, very spontaneous. If she had to point out a flaw in him it would be that he had a bad case of back acne but she never found it at all repulsive, barely noticing it after the first time she saw him naked. They were both in relationships when they met but for some reason it did not matter. It did not matter in the least because they were living a summer of destiny all their own. They were blind to anything that did not fit neatly into their time together and they could not stay apart for more than a day or two during the entire semester. They were kindred spirits brought together for a brief moment in time. They knew without knowing that their time was limited and they made the best of it, not wasting one moment to any negative thought or hesitation. They shared food while hanging out in her dorm suite listening and singing to her music collection. They danced together inside the dorm and outside on the streets in sections of the campus housing not utilized during the summer and supposedly closed to students. They danced and sang as they moved through the walkways that weaved through the campus housing buildings, laughing along the way. They learned that some of the halls in the closed campus sections were occupied because whenever they reached the end of one of the show tunes they sang as loudly as they were able, they heard some applause originating from somewhere inside.

That summer the college administration imposed strict dorm visitation and lock down rules that she and her lover thought were overly burdensome-they were cramping their social life. In a secret protest they purchased a box of disposable diapers, wrote the names of all the open summer dorms (starring their respective halls) then strung them together. They sneaked into the East Dining Hall after hours, stacked chairs on one of the large garbage bins, then with her standing on one of the chairs, her lover climbed onto her shoulders to reach the metal cast outline of the Nittany Lion from which he tied the diaper display end to end. The following day during meals they smiled and exchanged winks whenever they heard someone comment on their prank.

She and her best friend and lover played games all summer, closed down each of the local pubs and eateries at least once, explored the campus and everything it had to offer, and on a regular basis had the best casual, non-binding, non-committal sex. They were both sexually 'charged' and relied on each other to fulfill their hungry appetite. Their relationship would be called something like 'friends with benefits' in later day terms but that summer, they never tried to define their re-

50

lationship. It did not matter. It was what it was and they enjoyed each other fully. The summer brought one happy, carefree, spontaneous moment after another and proved to be one of the best of her life.

Chapter Seven
Instinct

On one of the rare occasions she was not with her lover she attended a party at one of the fraternity houses located on the edge of town. She had been to quite a few parties that summer (that is what you do after all) and once she even left her shoes and walked back to the dorms barefoot. The following day she retrieved them at the dorm mailboxes where someone was kind enough to leave them for her. At this party her shoes stayed on. She had fun meeting and talking with some new people, mostly upper graduate students and a few locals, but got separated from the girlfriend she went with and so found herself walking back to the dorms alone. She decided to take a short cut through a section of campus that was closed for the summer but that she knew well from her previous late night galavants.

As she walked up the unlit pathway she suddenly became aware of a change in her body. Her muscles tightened, especially in her abdomen and neck and her shoulders rose slightly. At first she thought that maybe the beer she drank was turning against her but she had not had enough to make her drunk, sick, or even give her a 'buzz'. She was not that big a fan of beer so only drank enough for sociability sake. She quickly dismissed the notion that the feeling she was experiencing was in any way related to what she had to drink. As she walked along again she felt herself tighten. She became more and more uneasy. She could not shake the bad feeling. It was as though her inner radar was trying to tell her something but she could not pick up the full signal. She slowed her walk and tried to force herself to relax. Just then she heard a male voice from behind her on a lower section of the path shout, "Hey!" She spun around in time to see a dark blur just a few feet away dash to her right and past a line of bushes. She could hear the movement of someone running away but could not see anyone or anything around the bushes or the darkened lawns beyond.

A couple was running up the path toward her and as she was still running, the girl blurted out, "Did you see that guy?" I shook my head and her companion added, "Yeah, we saw him follow you all the way from town. It looked like he pulled something out of his pocket and started to move toward you faster-that's why I yelled." He quickly added, "Why don't you walk with us the rest of the way." She took them up on the offer and they walked her safely to her dorm.

Later while replaying the events of that evening in her head, she contemplated the changes she had in her body while she was walking and wondered if they were linked in some way to her intuition or instinct. Were these changes in her body its way of sending her a message of possible danger? The concept of danger on campus was utterly absurd. What kind of danger could we possibly have here? This place is full of students, professors, administration, and townspeople, the likes of which are the kind that are made up of families who have been here for generations, well-rooted. Not to mention all the campus security. They are everywhere! No, there's no danger. The opposite really! We are overly protected, what with all the dorm security. They lock us in at night, have sign in/sign out monitors at the doors, require us to show our picture ids, and they don't even allow visitors after hours. Danger? Here? No, that does not make any sense at all. What that couple saw was probably some stupid kid who didn't want caught playing some stupid prank. The one haunting bit of information that did not fit her explanation was that the students escorting her agreed that the man they saw did not look like the other college students walking about town and that his actions seemed deliberate as they watched him follow her on the forked paths as she headed toward the dorms. If he was innocent, why run away when they called out? Why didn't he just turn around and face them?

Up to that point in her life she had never been fearful of anything really. The doors to her childhood home were rarely locked, she walked by herself everywhere without concern and she was generally trusting of others. Why wouldn't she trust everyone? What would anyone ever possibly have against her? Why would anyone, anywhere ever want to do her harm? She had never hurt anyone, ever, so why would anyone want to hurt her? It made no logical sense to her and at that time in her life anything that did not make sense was simply dismissed.

Even though she was generally trusting of people, she was not totally naive about life. She was aware that some people would take advantage if they had the opportunity and there were criminals living freely, waiting and watching for their next opportunity, their next victim. She mostly learned that from a distance, through books, radio and television news broadcasts, entertainment programs and movies with story lines that included 'bad guy' type characters. It was nonetheless true that she was somewhat sheltered in her childhood and had not the advantage other 'street smart' kids had when it came to sizing up people. That is a skill she learned the hard way, through the stream of disappointments she experienced when realizing she could not always rely upon the word of another. She had never been confronted by anyone or anything threatening harm in the past but that summer she began to question her safety. She questioned whether or not she was secure and she wondered if she would instinctively know what to do to protect herself if necessary. Would she know to stand strong or to flee?

In an article titled Fight or Flight published on the website Science How Stuff Works, Julia Layton writes that we have two systems the brain activates to produce the fight-or-flight response. The sympathetic nervous system that uses nerve pathways to initiate reactions in the body like muscle tension, and the adrenal-cortical system that uses the bloodstream. The affect of the former results in an alert body. On the latter, when the pituitary gland is triggered to secrete the hormone ACTH (adrenocorticotropic hormone), ACTH moves through the bloodstream and at the adrenal cortex, activates the release of approximately 30 different hormones that prepare the body to deal with a threat. The reaction includes increase heart rate, pupil dilation to allow us to see the maximum amount of light, and the shut down of nonessential body functions to allow more energy for emergency functions.

So it seems that the body is equipped to handle a response to fear but what causes fear? In the same article Julia Layton goes on to explain that the process of creating fear takes place subconsciously in the brain. The process involves two separate streams of thought taking place simultaneously. When a stimulus event occurs, the first stream triggers an immediate response, a "Run for your life now!" type of reaction and the second is slower and more deliberate, considering various facts that provide other possible explanations to what is taking place and therefore more options for reaction. Both streams lead to the same place in the brain that triggers the flight-or-fight response.

If she had been following national news of missing women a year earlier, she would have been justified if she was afraid and untrusting even though she was on a seemingly safe college campus that summer.

While she was still in high school young women in Portland and Seattle were disappearing from college campuses. At the time she was experiencing all the joys of high school senior year a man no one thought capable was committing horrific bad acts near to a college campus in the Salt Lake City area. He preyed on unsuspecting young women who were captivated by his charm and good looks and were taken in by his deceptive acts of helplessness. He would put on a fake cast and carry books across campus then purposely drop them when a pretty coed was walking nearby. Then he would entice her to his car where he would kidnap her then take her to where he would rape, murder, and then dump her tortured body. The one victim who was able to escape reported that he was wearing a police uniform when he kidnapped her from a Utah mall parking lot. Ted Bundy's arrest was due, in part, to that brave and lucky woman's ability to describe items (including a pair of handcuffs he used on her) that she saw in his car. These items were later found by police when they stopped Bundy for traffic violations.

The year Bundy was arrested for the kidnap of the woman who escaped his terror, she and a friend from college decided to head south for the winter season. They had pre-arranged work at a tourist vacation resort around Daytona Beach, Florida but ended up going further south to a popular spring break destination and the promise of warmer weather. While her friend made an abrupt decision to return north before the end of the season, she decided to stay, having landed a steady office job that came with a new group of friends.

During that first year on her own the television stations aired news about a series of killings. They were dubbed 'canal murders' because bodies were discovered in the canals extending inland off the intracoastal waterway. She kept her eyes peeled on the waters below whenever walking across a bridged canal at night and during those walks began to rethink her decision to remain in Florida. That year was the first year she spent the Christmas Holiday alone which was extremely difficult at the time. She walked past houses with lights in the window and sometimes could hear laughter and music floating through the air. Laughter and music that sounded so inviting but was not because she was outside and alone. She forced herself to move past it, telling herself that it was building her character, making her stronger.

Over the next year she worked in real estate property management by day and ran with the elite club crowd by night, where she met a guy with whom she would share many intimate moments, including grief over the loss of 'The King'.

Five months later Bundy, now dubbed with the nicknames 'Lady Killer' and 'The Campus Killer' escaped captivity for a second time then broke into a Chi Omega Sorority house at Florida State University on January 14, 1978, attacking four young women, killing two. She was still in Florida and beginning to feel disillusioned by the failing business she had started the previous fall while she waited for results of the broker exam.

Launching a new business is never easy but the lack of communication from her business partner doomed theirs from the start. Her instinct had warned her that a relationship with this man was not a good idea, but she continued down a playful path, following her girlish emotions. She had left a promising relationship to chase after what would turn out to be an illusion of love and friendship. She lived in a riddle, each day trying to figure out the meaning of their conversations and what intrigued her at the beginning grew tiresome. She found that she was going through motions that were meaningless to her and when she asked questions about the future she was not given any real information. She felt like she was just drifting along spellbound without any purpose, used, like a pawn. She was beginning to lose her sense of identity and could not help but think she was caught up in someone else's hidden agenda. There were too many contradictions between what she heard and what she witnessed. She thought she was falling in love;

but she had known love and this relationship, whatever it was, was not love. She was young and inexperienced. She waited for guidance that never came and felt that she had to fake understanding the world of business when she was really clueless. Fake by silence. Fake through cooperation. She faked it until she reached a point where she could not bear it any longer. She needed to escape from living in the dark, from what she felt was a sham existence. If she had listened to her instincts at the start she would have avoided the mistake of that relationship and all the heartbreak that followed but the heart wants what the heart wants.

She wondered if any victims of misguided experiences hear an inner voice pulling at them or shouting some warning? If their instinct picked up on something would they have simply dismissed it because outward appearances assured them they had nothing to fear? How do we instinctively know at times to avoid a certain person or situation if everything in the scenario appears normal and safe? Do we hear and see only the things we want to hear and see or is what we hear and see the full spectrum of what we can comprehend? After many years she came to understand that it may be possible to feel beyond what we can see and can possibly avoid disastrous future events if we take heed to our inner intuition/instinct.

Before she could trust her instinct she had to understand denial and acceptance. Sometimes we avoid negative news because at that point in time we simply do not want to face whatever it is. We wallow in denial, secretly hoping that if we ignore the truth it will go away and by ignoring it we have the power to alter reality. We can shield ourselves for a short while; however the realization that we cannot alter past events will creep in eventually and we will be forced to face the truth.

Years later, she knew that her father had died before she received the phone call and when the call came she refused to answer it. She refused because she was not ready to hear the news that would confirm what she already knew. She was not ready. She stayed in denial. In her mind, every hour she remained in denial delayed the truth, but what she was not ready to accept at the time was that the truth was already set. He was dead. It was time for acceptance. She was so aggrieved that she missed the extraordinary event-her instinct revealed the truth. After her fathers death she began to accept that her instincts were strong and they revealed the truth. She started to turn to her inner self, her quiet self and in the years to follow she came to understand the importance of paying attention when she experienced an uneasy feeling.

One Saturday morning she was driving on a freeway with her young teenage daughter, who, noticing the air bag warning on the front passenger dash, insisted on sitting in the back where she fell asleep less than twenty minutes into the drive. While navigating over a steep incline she suddenly had an uneasy feeling. They were heading to the beach but had to drive over a local mountain range to get there. The freeway had numerous lanes but was winding and steep in some sections. The weather was good and the road conditions were favorable. Still, she had an uneasy feeling and the muscles around her stomach tightened. She gripped the steering wheel tighter and as her shoulders rose slightly and her neck stiffened, she began to focus intently on the road ahead. She searched her memory for anything in her life that may be the source of some 'happening' the likes of which would cause such an uneasy feeling. These feelings always accompanied a negative event of some sort-bad news or a bad experience. The fact that they were moving at over 65 miles an hour on a multi-lane freeway was not lost on her-she slowed down. Then it occurred to her that she should move out of the lane she was in. There was no reason to do so because there was no traffic directly in front of her slowing and no traffic in the other lanes to her right or left. She just 'knew' that she had to move, NOW! She steered to the right and as she did so narrowly missed hitting a large metal ladder, the likes of which she had regularly seen attached to the top of construction vehicles. The ladder was lying across the lane she had previously been traveling in and was partially in the lane farther to the left. Had she not moved when she did she would not have been able to navigate around it. She shuddered when realizing how close she came to catastrophe. She drove on and once she composed herself completely she realized that the uneasy feeling was gone. Message received.

Chapter Eight
The Coordinates

♂

After her first attempt at business failed her life was filled with the usual highs and lows most people experience. While living on the West coast of Florida she discovered the fun of oyster shucking parties, learned to stay clear of almond liquor, and fell in lust-love was too much to ask at the time- with a man who sailed chartered yachts around the world. He was the first man who was completely honest with her and she appreciated that, and that he never, ever, balanced his check- book. She found that fascinating because she was so anal about hers. He was not a suit type and that was a good change for her. He looked like Eric Clapton which made him a 'chick magnet,' but she didn't mind. If he had his way he would have invited them along, but she wasn't into that kind of thing. She was curious though and after confessing that she had never seen a porno flick he understood why. On that, she talked him into taking her to see one just for the experience so on a Satur- day afternoon they went. Following her usual movie going ritual, she bought popcorn before they found seats in the near- ly empty theatre. The title was something like, 'Babes in Space' and if there was a plot at all, she never figured it out. Just as well because they walked out after the film broke for the third time. They dated until he moved away to run a yacht dealership in Texas. She visited once but did not consider fol- lowing him because she still held a torch for her old business partner and was drawn back to the opposite coast.

Once she was established in a decent job, she started to date again and met her future husband during a Friday happy hour. He was very handsome (looked like a combination of

61

Kurt Russell and Paul Newman), charming, self-assured, and totally swept her off her feet. Their relationship moved quickly along and they were engaged for marriage within eighteen months. During their time together they had a blast with some of the best people she had ever met. The ultimate experience they shared, one that she considered spectacular compared to all the others, was parenthood.

She had quite a few amazing experiences in her life leading up to this point but nothing compared to her joy when she became a mother. There was something so special about that, like waking up each day with the realization that she won some fantastically grand prize. She felt a love unlike any other and she was extremely happy in that love. The love of being a mother opened up love to her on a new level, a deeper and more purposeful level.

It was only after giving birth and experiencing this deep love that her sense of intuition seemed to reboot and continue to develop as before; however not immediately after. For at least six weeks after childbirth she was forgetful, slow in her thinking, and at times struggled to put a coherent sentence together. Lack of rest and hormonal shift were the logical causes. She should have rested when her newborn slept but instead she used that time to do household chores and prepare for the baby's awakening. She should have taken a longer time from work but felt she had a duty to her customers waiting anxiously for their loan approvals (she actually spoke with a customer while still in the hospital). She felt accountable for her work and to the bank loan manager and the expectations placed on her to meet the monthly sales quota. She was also motivated by a conversation she had with her sales manager when in her last trimester. She wanted to take on additional responsibility and let him know she was interested in an upcoming promotional opportunity. The response she received was that she would not be considered because he naturally assumed that she would not return to her job once her baby was born. In those days managers could still say things like that, even in a conservative bank. She wanted to show him that the job was important to her and so returned within three weeks, obtaining a doctor's note to do so. She also wanted to continue breastfeeding and that decision brought with it the need to pump milk in the office restroom and at times nonchalantly reach into her suit coat jacket to squeeze her leaking nipples during a staff meeting.

Once she fully recovered she felt invincible-there is nothing to stop a woman once she has been through childbirth! She was acutely aware of her newly acquired ability to focus and resolve issues. Her marriage did not last but she was determined to maintain some of the relationships she had established with her extended family and friends. It was easier said than done. There is something really strange that happens to some people when friends or a family member divorce. They feel they have to choose between the separated pair and sometimes the choice is based on who had established the friendship first. That was hard for her because at the time of their split the majority of their friends were friends with him first. She was starting over with just a few friends close by. She was starting over and was responsible for the wellbeing of another tiny person who had to come first. The banking industry was suffering through mergers and acquisitions, closures, and stagnant lending. In several states building projects were abandoned shells and work in her field was suddenly not available. She reached out for family support and found it in her loving sister so moved herself and her daughter to Pennsylvania and the promise of steady employment.

She felt that she needed to bolster her credentials in order to assure a stable livelihood so she added college coursework to her already tight schedule. She worked full time while completing her undergraduate degree and spent every free moment with her daughter. Time was a precious commodity in her life and she learned to use it wisely. She would think about a decision she had to make or some unresolved issue while she was performing some other task. She found that the best time to do this was during exercise. The distraction of thinking about anything was welcomed as she toiled away on the treadmill. She would look out the health club window and focus on the trees outside and let her mind wrap itself around whatever she needed to resolve. One Saturday afternoon she was thinking about her housing situation and while she gazed at a tree some leaves and branches took the shape of a miniature version of herself, her daughter, and a puppy neatly entwined together as branch extension. She blinked, expecting it to disappear but the vision only became clearer, with more detail. She saw a yard and flowering bushes at the front of the nest. In her mind she thought, "Focus on the nest." Within six months she engaged a realtor to help find their new home.

Her daughter seemed happy with all the different potential purchases, finding some little spot in each one where she would set up whatever treasures she brought along that day as if to make herself at home there. The one eventually chosen was not on the list the realtor had brought with her that sunny cool Saturday in March. As the realtor drove them around in an area they had never been before, she suddenly asked the realtor what was at the top of a particular street they were approaching. The realtor indicated it was a nicely established neighborhood and made a turn to drive up the street. As they drove further into the development and approached a corner stop sign she spied a 'for sale' sign in front of the perfect ranch house with flowering bushes lining the front patio. The house sat on a lot with a sloping front yard, a deep back yard and was adjacent to a corner lot where the school bus stopped. During their walk through her daughter claimed one of the bedrooms hers by putting her treasures on the window sill and as they explored the property she continually referred to it as "Home." They closed escrow before Mother's Day.

The first day in the new house was a happy one in spite of all the physical work involved. She wanted this for her daughter and for herself too. She knew she was exactly where she ought to be and there was a sense of peace in that. That night she was still enjoying the satisfaction of knowing she achieved her goal when another thought, one she did not at all expect, crossed her mind-They will come tonight. They will most assuredly come because they have to come. They have to come to get the coordinates. They will come tonight to get the coordinates because they always do.

She knew they always came when she moved to a new location and she also knew that she always forgot about it afterward. She knew when it was happening if she was awake to witness it but still she always forgot afterward. It was just a normal part of the move, like calling the utility company to turn on the electric service. It was ordinary so why think about it?

That night, partly because she was energized with the excitement of being in her new home and partly because she was curious why that earlier thought crossed her mind this time when she could not recall that happening previously, she decided to stay awake and try to witness the event. There were two windows in her bedroom, each set into walls adjacent to each other, one looked out into the fenced in part of the back-yard and the other the side yard and large pines with roots that spread through the yard reaching as far as the flat concrete stone slabs sitting just beyond her kitchen entrance door. She left the bedroom curtains open and laid on her back in bed staring out and up at the sky.

She nearly fell asleep waiting but her patience paid off when she saw the orb hovering at her window. There it was. She stretched up to see it better-It looked like it was made of a dull copper color metal but it was a bit lighter in color than a copper penny. Different this time, she knew without knowing how she knew, she just did. This one was different. It hovered outside her window for just about few seconds before a slit opened up and a light beamed from the orb into the bedroom, hitting the wall to the left of her closet and spanning the distance to cover the bedroom door. She looked back and forth between the orb and the beam of light like watching a tennis match, waiting for something to happen. The slit in the orb closed after just a few seconds more but the beam of light shining in the room lingered. While she was focused on the light the Orb shot off or disappeared, she was not sure, it was just gone when she turned her gaze back to where it hovered. Her mind was puzzling over the lingering beam-How could a beam of light linger this way? This was really strange. She switched her gaze back to the section of door and wall where the light beam lingered and then back to the window. The orb was definitely gone but here was this light still shining. The light beam remained constant, like a moon beam, only there was no visible moon in the sky. The sky was clouded over and the air thick and misty with the aftermath of a late spring rain that swept through earlier that evening. Still the light lingered, shining steadily against the wall and door but now there was no diagonal beam extending from near the window. There was just a lit section, like the target of a spotlight but without the beam shining from the light.

The light must be coming in from somewhere outside. She reassured herself that a logical explanation to this must exist. A light cannot shine without its source. The source of this light has to be somewhere.

She proceeded to search for the source. She looked out both windows but did not see anything helpful to solve the mystery. She went to the door and put up her hands to block the light and saw her shadow against the door. She opened the door and saw that the light now reflected against the hallway wall. She closed the door and returned to her bed feeling an overwhelming pull to sleep.

Sometime later she awoke to find that the light was gone, replaced by the saturating shine of the full moon no longer hidden by cloud cover. The moon shifted from the Western sky to the East and it was now brightly shining through her bedroom window that faced out to the backyard.

Chapter Nine
Angel Dog

⚓

Soon after moving into the house she indulged her daughter with a pure breed Australian shepherd puppy, a tricolor red merle that caught her daughters eye by hesitating shyly when the other puppies were falling all over themselves to get noticed. She had one chestnut brown eye and one blue eye and had a distinctive marking of an angel in the fur on her right side. They named her Ondi Andrea on her papers, but called her Onnie and before long she found herself regularly purchasing a new stake and lead for the back yard, each one thicker, with hopes that Onnie would not be strong enough to break it. No such luck! Onnie was extremely strong and always broke the leads. Whenever she broke free from her back yard run Onnie would 'round up' the neighborhood, chasing all the outside cats she could find, then eventually make her way back to the house, usually planting herself on the front porch where she waited for them to return. Their fear was that during one of Onnie's galavants the lead line still attached to her collar would catch on a fence or that Onnie would get stuck under a car while chasing a cat, but to their relief nothing ever happened to Onnie that a good soapy bath would not remedy.

She had taken the advice of Onnie's breeder to maintain a large pen in the house, used mostly at night and while Onnie was still training, when they left the house for the day. The pen had a metal gate door that could be latched in a closed lock position; however they rarely used the latch lock. Sometimes Onnie would close herself in (usually when she had misbehaved and knew it) but if either she or her daughter closed the gate with Onnie inside Onnie would always push it open just a little as soon as they left the room.

Onnie girl was the perfect addition to their little family and she soon took on the role of protector. Aussies are notably protective and Onnie lived up to this reputation. The first time they witnessed it was on Halloween when her daughter was opening the door to a group of trick-or-treaters and Onnie suddenly leaped up and grabbed her daughters arm in her mouth and pulled her away from the door. For a dog that once protested a walk around her new neighborhood by putting her front paws down and holding her legs stiff so to prevent her from moving forward, Onnie had made a huge leap-she found her courage that night and they were proud of her.

Once trained, Onnie could be trusted to roam the house all day, but other than sleeping on the living room sofa she stayed mostly in the kitchen where the vinyl flooring was cooler. The kitchen was a great vantage point because it had a large window near the table and chairs that looked out over the front porch, and lawns. Onnie would balance her front legs up onto a kitchen chair where she could look out the window and bark at the mail carrier or any other person or animal she saw. One exception to this was the dog next door. Onnie met that dog when she was a pup so did not seem to mind if the dog breached the property line. Not so with the new dog across the street who was about a fourth of Onnie's size. That dog would play a little game with Onnie. It ran to the kitchen door, scratched at it, barked and then ran back across the street. A doggy version of 'tag-you're it!' That drove Onnie nuts! That, and the occasional glimpse of a mole. The neighborhood yards were full of their networked tunnels. If Onnie caught sight or scent of one in the backyard she would dig a hole. The yard section nearest to the neighbors fence was a mine field of mole holes courtesy of Onnie.

69

Long before Onnie's first birthday they had all three grown quite attached. The bond between them went deeper than she had ever knew possible. She had pets before but Onnie was more a member of the family than a pet. When they were leaving on an out of town vacation and needed to board Onnie for the week, they reluctantly took her to a boarding facility on the fringe between the outlying suburbs and the country. It was one of those places that had individual runs and private pens for the boarded animals, daily schedules that included plenty of play time, and spoil with promises of regular treats. After dropping Onnie off they drove home and were glad they had all the last minute things to do to keep busy. They missed her already.

Later that night, after all the final packing, checking and rechecking their travel itinerary, getting her daughter to bed, assuring that the alarm was properly set, she finally fell asleep, but not for long. Sometime in the middle of the night she awoke suddenly thinking she heard Onnie's shrill bark, the one she made when she was outside and wanted to come in. She thought she heard movement in the kitchen and got up to explore the source of the noise. When she got to the kitchen she felt Onnie. She felt her presence as sure as if she was right there in front of her and as she knelt down she felt the body slam-Onnie's trade mark body slam that rocked her backward onto her heels. She had no explanation for the experience and was at first distressed thinking that perhaps something happened to Onnie and it was her spirit visiting. Perhaps she just dreamt the whole thing and it was that kind of dream, the most vivid kind that made it feel so real that it rocked her consciousness and triggered apprehension. Onnie was in her boarder's pen at the time she felt her presence at the house. How was that possible? How could she be in two places at the same time but for some stronger than understood invisible thread of love or consciousness? Could such a thing even exist? She had heard that a strong bond exists between mothers and their children but is it possible to build a strong bond with an animal? If anyone asked she would say yes, definitely yes it is.

Chapter Ten
The Return

♂

Since childhood she had suffered with two afflictions, low blood pressure, the cause of more than one fainting incident, and car motion sickness triggered by attempts to read anything longer than a line or two of text while riding in the back seat of a moving vehicle. Not all motion bothered her. When she was very young she was unaffected by circular motion. She could spin herself round long enough that the world around her seemed to tilt and lurch when she stopped, lost balance, then tumbled softly to the grass beneath her feet. The fun of spinning round until losing balance lost its luster for her sometime in her adolescence stage. As she grew older she found that she had a declining tolerance for exposure to circular motion in general. Her stomach would lilt for at least twenty minutes afterward. There were two exceptions. Riding on a bobbing Merry-Go-Round horse and spinning on a local amusement park ride called The Rotor. The Rotor was a tube-like room where the riders stood shoulder to shoulder with their backs up against the thickly padded circular wall. The room spun around faster and faster until it spun so fast that when the floor dropped-the climax of the ride-all the riders were held to the wall by centrifugal forces winning against gravity.

As she grew older her fainting incidents lessened, in part because she was no longer required to kneel for long periods in church. She had fainted often enough there that she was made to sit next to the sister (nun) which totally spoiled any fooling around fun she could have had. The only up side was that she was no longer frowned upon if she chose to half sit, half kneel during the long kneel only sections of mass. She also learned what to do if she felt she was getting light-headed-put her head between her knees until the feeling passed. If she wasn't in church she could eat something salty to raise her blood pressure which always worked.

She had heard of vertigo but never understood the seriousness of it until one Autumn Saturday evening as she sat watching a television program with her middle school age daughter. She had made stuffed cabbage for dinner and with the cabbage leafs too small to stuff, a bowl of cole slaw. After dinner she tasted the cole slaw before refrigerating it, intending to enjoy it the following day but that never came to fruition. She had mixed what she later believed was rancid mayonnaise in the cole slaw recipe and within just a short time after the dinner clean up, while sitting on the sofa when the room, the entire room began to spin around. Literally, spin around. There is no way to truly describe how it looks without going through it but if you have ever been standing in a 360 degree surround theatre with a moving image projected on the walls around you that is the only experience that comes close. She immediately felt sick to her stomach and stumbled her way to the bathroom where she would remain on the floor, half hung over the side of the bathtub (she could not make it as far as the commode) through the rest of the night and into the wee hours of the morning. Once she had expelled all food and bile from her system she lay there with dry heaves, still not able to move her body. Each time she tried the room would start to spin again. She could not even open her eyes. So she stayed there until she fell asleep. After waking an hour or two later she crawled with her eyes closed on her hands and knees, feeling her way into her bedroom while dragging a bucket across the floor. It was all she could do to get herself up into her bed. She laid on her back and did not move the entire day; however later in the early afternoon she was finally able to open her eyes for a short time. If she kept them opened long enough to focus on anything she naturally turned her head and with even the slightest movement the spinning resumed. So she lay there, listening to the sounds outside and periodically called out words of assurance and instruction to her daughter.

The next day, with the help of her daughter she telephoned her work from her bed and told them the situation. They sent a car to pick her up and drove her to the hospital where she underwent a physical exam and CAT scan, and received medication that gave her restless legs but helped her fully recover. She carried around a filled prescription bottle with the medication for several years in fear of experiencing another episode of vertigo; however it never repeated, though on occasion, mostly in the morning hours following a transport return, she did have mild motion sickness symptoms. On the transport itself her memory is not at all clear so it is impossible to distinguish what may be dream recollection. In one instance she was waiting with at least one other person, a male, who was hesitating from climbing into a cylinder shaped body tube, similar to the type of tube commonly found in a bank drive through. She brushed past him and said, "I'll go." She bent down to clear the overhead as she climbed into the tube and waited for the hatch to close. She put herself in a yoga type pose, leaning forward over her folded legs beneath her tucking her head in front with both arms reaching back along the sides. She closed her eyes and fell unconscious at the instant she felt movement.

Sometimes there were holding stations where she and others would wait. She sat watching as some people shuffled around the room while others passed through entry and exit ways. Some were dressed in pajamas (she stopped sleeping naked after that) and on occasion she would see someone dressed in a green pilot jumpsuit.

74

She has some memory of what she believes may be the very end of returning, when she is gaining full consciousness. Several times a year, usually on a Friday or Saturday night when the moon was full, she woke to feel and sometimes see what may have been the remnants of some form of travel.

Sometimes she felt a turntable beneath her body. She felt it as clearly as if she had placed it there herself. She could even feel it move. It shifted slightly like a 'Lazy Susan' would when you spin it round to find the spice you need then stop it suddenly when you see the spice there before you. When the turntable steadies it pivots backward just a bit because it is still in inertia spin. That's how it felt, her body suddenly, smoothly stopped into a final position. She could feel the shift, a movement beneath her, then nothing at all, like it vaporized into thin air.

Once, only once that she could recall, she awoke to see and feel what appeared to be a cold metal talon running the width of her stomach from right to left. She could see the gleam of the metal as it lightly grazed over her smooth middle and watched as it vanished into thin air when it completed the crossing.

At other times she awoke early enough to see some kind of matter covering her body. The nature of the covering changed somewhat over the years but at first it was visible to her, even in wee hours of darkness with only as much beam of moonlight shining through as the opaque curtains allowed. It was thick enough to secure her body-she knew without knowing that it held her in place during travel, like a baby is held in a womb. She could see some rippling movement so knew it was flexible and she saw it was somewhat transparent, though not as clear as glass. It looked thick like mercury or some kind of plasma and reminded her of what the alien in the movie Predator looked like when it hid itself in the jungle-you could see it if you really looked because its form distorted the background imagery even though it was transparent. Yes, it looked exactly like that. She could still envision the weightless blanket of fluid-like matter receding from her, moving downward, slowly, methodically pulling away from her as though it were melting. As it lifted from her body it melted into nothing and when the last of it was gone she realized she was fully awake but felt no fear.

Of course it is absolutely possible she was lucidly dreaming during this and the fluid a metaphor of her dream like state melting away. She has had experiences where she woke up while in a dream and the dream kept playing, so she kept her eyes closed and watched a bit more of it play out, like watching a movie, but as she became more alert, the sound and picture faded and she lost the dream to full consciousness. This just felt different, mostly because her eyes were not closed.

During the experience it never occurred to her to try and touch the osculating and transparent blanket that encased her body when she returned. The thought never entered her mind while it was happening. She doubted her ability to do so even if she had wanted to because she believed that most of her body was in a semi paralyzed state.

A few times she awoke because she felt herself hard hit the bed, like she was dropped there. Those hard landings can be explained by Earthquakes because a similar jarring affect happens when Earthquakes result from plates shifting. She should have kept a journal of the dates to check this but did not, so rather than accept that she would be so haphazardly handled, she chooses to believe the jolts were at the hand of mother nature.

She recalled that the position of her body was always the same on the return. She was flat on her back her head straight forward, her legs straight forward, and her arms bent to allow her hands to cross one over the other on the top of her chest. The body positioning was similar to the Egyptian mummy inside the take apart model set she had purchased for her daughter at a science toy store.

While her daughter was young, she would naturally think of her after having a return type experience knowing that she lay sleeping in her room across the hall. If the door to her bedroom was open she could catch Onnie cross the hall from her daughters room into the living room. If she listened closely she could hear Onnie enter her pen, shuffle herself around to a comfortable position, and finally, the light clang of the pen gate as it hit the side of a kitchen chair when Onnie gave it a final push open.

Chapter Eleven
The Transport

Her journey to understanding the transport began with a limited understanding of common scientific principles as applied to what she perceived in her everyday world coupled with the experiences she had with the Grays, most of which usurped those same principles.

First, she learned that both the Small Grays and Tall Grays have unique vision abilities. They can see and project what they 'see' beyond what we know as visible light. When they do this they are either seeing through, for example, a solid wall or projecting an image onto a wall that appears as such. One Small Gray demonstrated this to her while they stood alone in a four walled room. The Gray gestured for her to look at the blank wall and when she did she was able to see beyond it (or an image projected onto it) that showed another room with several Small Grays working in what looked like a science lab or examining room. With a simple wave of their hand the wall changes back to its original appearance. So what is that? Hypnosis or what? She was a non-believer but that changed when the Gray walked her through an opening and there was the same scene, live, up close and personal. Even though she could not explain it she could not discount it either. It just was.

Their vision abilities are evolved to the point where they appear to detect light along the length of what is currently defined as the total light spectrum, from Gamma rays to Radio waves, though they are not seeing in the same sense as we see when they see beyond visible light. They seem to pick up waves using visual and auditory senses.

In terms of light wave energy detection, the shorter wavelengths have higher amounts of energy and of the three categories of infrared light the near infrared is closest to visible light. As a point of reference, mid infrared waves, used in remote control devices, have a range beginning at the long end of the near infrared wave-1.3 microns which is 1,300 billionths of a meter to a length of 3 microns and the longest of the three, the thermal infrared, can extend up to 30 microns. While it may seem logical that the Grays would detect the near infrared waves, it is much more plausible they would detect thermal infrared since those waves are the most abundant and it is not necessary to have a precision point of reflection. Thermal infrared is detected through the energy emitted from an object rather than by reflecting off it. A special lens is used to detect the detailed temperature pattern (a thermogram) from objects in view and the output is a color intensive image.

So was she really seeing just what the Grays wanted her to see, some projected reality of the Grays' making or was she seeing or dreaming the reality of another place or dimension beyond the third?

Was it possible to actually change the molecular structure so as to travel along an otherwise unattainable energy pathway then change back to a solid form again? If this is possible what would that pathway look like? Not light waves because they are generally not very strong, right? Or would that even matter if the molecular change resulted in a long stretched out version of former self, easily pulled at one end but held strong together like the links of a chain? Was there an actual physical change at all or was it just a transformation in the brain? Was the transport a form astral projection or an application of quantum mechanics?

On the former, she did not hold much credence because it logically just did not make much sense. If it was possible, why wasn't it a standard mode of transportation? She just could not get her mind wrapped around the concept without leaning toward the camp that held the experience to be nothing more than lucid dreaming. Benjamin Rathord, deputy editor of Skeptical Inquirer science magazine opines that while the astral projection pastime can seem profound it is nothing more than an entertaining pastime and there is no evidence that the experiences happen outside the body instead of inside the brain. Scientists reject astral projection for lack of evidence of a soul or that a consciousness can exist outside the brain. Applying Occam's Razor, the principal that states if there are different theories to explain a phenomenon the simplest one, with the least assumptions is likely the correct answer, in the case of astral projection, dreaming would win out over leaving the body.

On the latter, quantum mechanics, there is a relatively new theory that may hold the key—String theory. In his article on string theory Alberto Güijosa describes the Standard Model of particle physics as "the fundamental building blocks of which all the world is made and the forces through which these blocks interact." There are twelve basic building blocks (six quarks: up, down, charm, strange, top, bottom and six leptons: electron, muon, talon and three neutrinos) that produce four forces (gravity, electromagnetism, weak nuclear and strong nuclear) when acting as carriers, like when photons are exchanged by two objects creating a magnetic attraction. The fundamental particles making up the four forces are gravitons, photons, three particles, W+, W- and Z and gluons, respectively.

The string theory premiss is that all the fundamental particles making up the Standard Model of particle physics are all just varied manifestations of one object-a string. So if the string oscillates one way it is a photon, another way, it is a quark, etc. String theory may provide a more accurate description than the Standard Model because although the Standard Model precisely describes the behaviors of most particles and forces it does not work to describe the force of gravity because gravity cannot be described microscopically; however all particles and forces can be described with precision when applying string theory to an extension of the model.

So if the behavior of gravity's particles-gravitons oscillate like a string is it possible to manipulate the oscillation in such a manner as to create a vertical no gravity or low gravity tube or tunnel in the Earth's atmosphere? Can photon particles be oscillated between objects in such a manner as to increase the force of electromagnetism?

Perhaps travel is possible through tapping into the strong magnetic telluric energy waves referred to as ley lines. Ley lines circumvent the Earth underground and through waters. Telluric energy currents originate with the rotation of the Earth which creates electric currents and results in a magnetic field on the surface that is further induced by the effects of the sun's radiation. Solar radiation is optimal at sunrise and sunset and therefore the telluric currents will magnetize on the Earth's surface at that time. Considering this, it is of no surprise to her that whatever the transport, she always, without exception, returned just before dawn

Chapter Twelve
Communication

平

We communicate through many methods, sometimes orally through the use of words and other times through the gestures we make. Words we choose during conversation may trigger a feeling in the listener such that cuts to the core of the listener's emotion, invoking a more emotionally charged response. The pace of our speech, the use of inflection, and the tone we use can enhance or end the effectiveness of our communication. If we speak slowly and in a monotone voice the listener may be lulled to a sleep-like state out of boredom. On contrast, if we speak hurriedly and with fear in our voice we may invoke apprehension in our audience and they may be inclined to end the conversation prematurely in an effort to separate themselves from the speaker.

On the use of body gestures, even the simplest one can be interpreted differently, sometimes without a change in the circumstances. A nod of the head may mean agreement, approval, acknowledgment of presence or just that we are paying attention to what the speaker is saying and we are encouraging him or her to continue.

There are universal body gestures, like a smile; however even a simple smile may not be genuine if the person smiling is doing so only to mask a hidden feeling. If the mouth is smiling but the eyes are not, the smiler is most likely not really smiling. The human eye retina will dilate when a person is interested or excited. The eyes seem to 'twinkle' when we are feeling happy or playful. People narrow their eyes when they are angered and widen them when surprised. There is a popular quote about the eyes from the bible (Matthew 6:22-23) that some trace back to Cicero who lived until 43 before Christ. This quote was later adopted by Shakespeare and transversed into the Chinese and English proverbs. The quote, "[T]he eyes are the window to the soul" is interpreted by most to mean that one can see the very depth of a person by looking into their eyes.

She could do something more with her eyes, something she learned when she was a child. She could make them move or shake from side to side very quickly. It was one of those odd things that she would share with friends when they all showed off what they could do, like wiggle their ears or disjoint their fingers or other extremities. Kids are weird like that. They take pride in their differences. As we age we tend to hide the same things we were so proud to show off as a kid but most people have something about them that is unique, aside from the obvious. Have you ever met someone who didn't have something different about them, flaw or gift?

Another odd thing she could do was allow one of her eyes to cross into the peripheral vision of the other. Sometimes this would happen naturally when she stared at an object for an extended period of time. The result was a shift in her vision line. Objects on the left moved to the right and they were superimposed upon each other so she could see double of half of what was on the left side. She was able to control her vision line and move the objects back and forth to create a space between the double image of both objects. She was able to manipulate the width of the space to expand and contract it. If she expanded the space and stared long enough at the center, sometimes patterns of color and light would appear and form shapes and images. The effect of moving her peripheral vision was quite different when she looked up into the night sky. She would see brighter flashes of light patterns that shifted and changed, all superimposed on the sky. She did not see any projected light beam originating from her or anywhere ground level that she could detect. The light was already there, in space, between the stars and while she held her gaze she was able to switch it on somehow. The light flashed similar to night lightning, except was concentrated in thin beams instead of a wide spreading flash. Sometimes it appeared as though the beams aligned with star patterns. There was more going on than just flashes of varying patterns of light in the sky. The light seemed to pulse and take on a rhythm like speech. As she thought of something she would see a pattern of light flash. She knew that she could not have been the source of the light, but it was strange that the light patterns coincidentally flashed while she was concentrating on a thought directed up at the stars. Stranger still, she felt there was a message in the light patterns, some communication meant for her at that moment. The patterns of light continued and she found that the changes corresponded with the expansion and contraction of the overlap space she was able to make when she shifted her peripheral vision. So, logically, the light patterns must have been some optical illusion. Still, she could not shake the feeling that something was attempting to communicate with her. She was fascinated with the experience but skeptical that it was anything more than a good optical illusion coupled with her active imagination. She had studied Logic in her undergraduate work and always looked for a scientific explanation to any unusual phenomena she experienced. This time she felt conflicted because a part of her was urging her to just go with it, experience it fully without stopping to question it. She was puzzled because the thoughts she had during the experience were like new ideas, creative ideas but such ideas did not correspond with her train of thought during the experience. She was not consciously seeking new ideas and this method did not follow her past creative patterns. In the past her creativity was spawned by some inspiration, a conversation, a good book, an experience. Ah! That was it! She was newly inspired by this experience and that was opening her mind to think creatively.

That was logical, right? So the creative process in her mind opened up as a way of explaining the optical illusion of light patterns; but what if? What if this could be a form of communication, like morse code that can be transmitted by using flashes of light?

She thought about a poem she wrote years earlier. The poem was about our thoughts. The underlying premiss of the poem was a question-Do our thoughts travel? In thinking about her experience with the optical illusion of the flashing light patterns she thought about the energy of light and movement. If everything we do produces energy, what about thinking? Are our thoughts a form of energy? If a thought is a form of energy is it projected energy? If it is projected energy where does it project to? Do our thoughts travel? If thoughts travel, like a wave of energy, where do they travel to and for how long? If thoughts project outward but bounce back to us like a rubber band do we store them in our memory, like in a vault, to be recalled and projected outward again? If a thought is not vocalized is it any less real? The answer is probably no to the person thinking it, right? An unvocalized thought is actually closer to reality than what is spoken if what is spoken is not the truth. Ever hear someone ask, "Did I just say that out loud?" If we can re-wire the path of neurons in the brain by consciously making an effort to think certain thoughts as discussed in Chapter Four, aren't the thoughts we transmit carrying the electrical signals when emerged from the electrochemical interactions of neurons? So if we recall a happy thought aren't we strengthening the neural pathway that triggers happy emotions? Is this why people who dwell over negative things don't seem to move past their own negativity?

Her thoughts while looking up at the shifting patterns of light were the kind one has while gazing at something interesting but unknown. Simply put, she was fascinated. Holding her gaze this way, probably close to being cross-eyed, took some effort and felt uncomfortable after a few minutes so she would end the experience by closing her eyes or abruptly looking away. When she opened her eyes and focused her gaze normally she could look up and see that the flashes would stop as did the flood of thoughts, the free thinking ideas that flowed into her brain during the experience.

She communicated with the creatures who came for her and the others she encountered under various circumstances during their visits together in one manner when they were close in proximity and it was always the same. The language was straightforward, simple and to the point. There were no ambiguities so no wasted time wondering if one or the other thing was meant. It was always crystal clear. She would think of a question if she needed or wanted to understand something and the creatures that seemed to be in charge of the situation-The Small Grays-would seem to respond immediately by looking at her then placing a responsive thought in her mind. Sometimes the Small Grays would anticipate her question and just place the answer for her in the usual manner. Ah! I was just going to ask that!

The communication she had with these beings grew more engaging over the years and covered a multitude of topics.

They expressed their desire to learn all they could about Earth, humans, the government systems and so on. It was not the basic knowledge of books that they wanted to learn from those who were engaged (she was not always the only human in the presence of a Small Gray). They did not need humans for that. They needed humans to learn the intricacies of the race, physical, mental, emotional, and spiritual. They struggled to understand the unique emotions humans have as individuals and why they change, sometimes for no apparent reason. The emotional front was the most difficult to grasp because individuality plays the lead. What drives humans to do what they do and what are they trying to accomplish? What do they expect to happen when they venture in one manner or another? Why do they get angry under one set of circumstances but not another that appear similar? What makes humans sad and what makes them happy? Why do some of them like something while others dislikes the same thing? What bonds some of them together while others are distant, distrusting or hurtful?

Well, good luck with that! She tried to explain the struggle, sometimes lifetime struggle that all humans go through to try and understand themselves, let alone others. Humans make great efforts to understand those people close to them, important in their lives but otherwise, generally, unless it is their professional calling, they resign themselves to the fact that they will never truly understand why people do what they do. Instead they learn how to interact socially and professionally, and if they are lucky, they meet someone with whom they can live with and share a lifetime of experiences. They develop and nurture deep love, which she viewed as the ultimate human success. The discussions about human nature and her personal shares on emotions were not at all lost on these creatures. At times she even felt they were trying hard to be empathetic to human feelings and emotions.

On one occasion she was taken to place that appeared to be the cockpit of a ship, though much bigger than that she had ever seen, even bigger than the jumbo commercial planes that fly across the pond. She saw instrument panels but they were unfamiliar and seemed to shift in and out of her focus. Then the Small Gray showed her some comfort advances they made in one of their craft chairs. When the Gray motioned for her to look at the new chair she heard the guide speak to her without speaking. In a matter-of-fact kind of tone she heard this thought: "Humans like to see where they're going." Ha! This is so true! Humans do like to see where they're going!

The improved design looked like a very expensive lounging chair. It was a dark colored elongated triangular shaped chair, similar to the shape of a dentist chair but deep set, almost like a body well. It had multiple ripple cushioning of some sort, like a fine soft leather, but did not have any odor. It had a head section that inclined slightly with sides that cushioned the ears on both sides. The head incline was much better than the old chair she thought (she did not know how she knew this) because it allowed for a forward view. Yes, Humans do like to see where they're going and I can definitely see ahead in this one.

Another memory takes her to a time when they were traveling on a craft and she could see ahead but could not move from her seat or for that matter any part of her body except her eyes-She insisted on that at one point. She would not allow them to cover her eyes or disable her from seeing if she was otherwise conscious. It was hard enough to remain still and know she could not move but she got used to it especially once she knew without knowing that if she stayed still during travel she was less likely to feel negative affects later. Now as she lay in the chair looking out over what seemed to be vast space, infinity, pure beauty-she was mesmerized, the Gray came to the side of the chair and she heard this thought, "Too bad you can't get frequent flyer miles." That one was too funny! It was the first joke she remembers one of them sharing and knew without knowing they were developing a deeper rapport. At that moment she could not help but feel a genuine sense of camaraderie. This creature actually understood and demonstrated a sense of humor. Furthermore it was able to grasp one of the most difficult aspects of joke telling-the delivery. She had only known a few people who were good at telling jokes and not making a living doing it. She was impressed.

88

There was much more to come though, more she would learn about their purpose. More importantly, she would learn how she and others would fit into the fulfillment of their shared destiny.

Chapter Thirteen
Evolution

✝

Some people like surprises. She was never a fan, not even of the good kind-they made her feel uncomfortable and she is not sure why. Maybe she was mislead as a child and carried emotional baggage. Whatever the reason, she did not tolerate being a part of any plan of action executed without her receipt of a roadmap beforehand. It did not bother her so much if the path of the road changed along the way or if events occurred that were unanticipated because she knew that even the best made plans could change. If there was a plan, and if something was expected of her, she insisted on knowing what was expected and why and the explanation had to make sense to her. She learned through personal growth sessions that her 'word' was 'understanding' and this is just one way the word resonated with her. When she had a doctor visit she insisted on receiving a 'play-by-play' of each act the physician or dentist performed beforehand. If there was any deviation in the execution she shut down and would not cooperate further in the process. When she was a young girl she went to the dentist and was mislead into believing that the drill would not hurt. When she suddenly felt a sharp pain she sprang up from the chair, darted across the room and locked herself in the bathroom. She refused to come out until her father promised to take her home. He did and by doing so began to regain her trust in him and his word. After that, anyone who wanted to gain her trust did so by doing what they said they were going to do or providing a sensible explanation if they acted otherwise. She was alert for deception in others and if she spotted it or discovered a hidden agenda, she would not make any attempt to deepen the relationship beyond that necessary to interact. If the interaction was a matter of choice, she would choose not to do so. When she was done she was done.

The interaction she had with the creatures who regularly came for her was no different in terms of her insistence on knowing their intentions and her need to understand. It was clear to her that they understood this on some level because although she had no recollection of asking them certain questions they nonetheless provided her with information that made her feel comfortable with the events that would unfold before her.

She insisted on knowing why they were here, why Earth why us. They answered by showing her the most depressing thing she had ever seen. In that one visit she instantly understood why. A Small Gray stood next to her and gestured with its left arm for her to look to her left. When she did so she saw before her a graveyard of some kind. The terrain was barren and bleak, void of any color other than a slightly darker than coin wrapper shade of brown. She saw what must have been thousands of them lying dead side by side, in wide and deep gorges, layer upon layer of them, all dead. She felt an overwhelming rush of sadness and could not think any thought or feel any other emotion while she stood there and looked out over the vast sea of dead creatures.

She gets a slight chill just recalling the feel of the Small Grays's arm when she reached over and touched it in a gesture of sympathy as she gazed in horror and sadness at the dead creatures shown to her. The creature was cool to the touch but did not warm when she held her hand on its arm. Instead, she began to get colder, a chill originating at the point of contact and slowly extending to the tips of her fingers and then outward from her hand to her wrist and spreading up her arm. She suddenly thought that if she did not pull away she would be unable to before long. She began to lose feeling in her hand and arm as the coldness continued to spread. As if by some force that put itself between her and the creature, she was pushed free. She slowly felt the return of blood to her arm now fallen to her side and though her fingers tingled she was able to wiggle them until the normal sensation was fully restored. She recoiled slightly and she felt a different kind of fear, like when you do something you know is wrong but are not sure of the consequences. You just know for certain that there will be consequences. She was confused. So that's why they're here-their kind has suffered some kind of mass destruction, but what does that have to do with us-How is this relevant to us?

The Small Gray answered as if she had spoken the question out loud. It told her that they did not have much time. The reason they were on Earth was because they were in search of a creature compatible on a molecular level for interbreeding. The interbreeding would not only benefit the Grays. It was also necessary in the interest of future planetary colonization to find whether or not the human species can survive as a hybrid. The Gray told her that the human species is favored as one worth saving. If humans cannot survive as a hybrid species there is a possibility that the species will face extinction because there is not enough time left for a normal evolutionary process. The Human race is worth saving, love is worth saving-that is what she was hearing. But saving from what?

The Earth is dying and now at a rate faster than humans may have the means to counter. As a race we have yet to fully conquer the ever-present natural diseases that ebb and flow like tides through pockets of the world. Despite all the technological advances made since the Industrial Revolution, especially those in the communication field, the majority of the population remains in a state of denial when it comes to the bleak reality regarding the diminishing state of planet

Earth. The simple fact is that human behavior is killing the Earth and it will die long before its natural cycle. If the planet is not destroyed in a nuclear war or a cosmic collision first, the use of fossil fuels and other emissions will continue to enhance the greenhouse effect resulting in irreversible changes to the planet that will cause catastrophic events, killing millions of its inhabitants. Global environmental disaster and viral pandemic are both real threats to the human race. The sad irony is that while man continues to rape the Earth of its natural resources, man is carelessly destroying lifeforms that may hold the potential to advance human knowledge of medicine and alternative energy sources, the likes of which may hold the key to finding a way to travel beyond the planet and seek a suitable refuge. The Grays could save a large number of humans by transporting them but they cannot determine the selective process. That is not their purpose.

If she agreed to be a donor she would be part of a new evolution and this evolution may not only preserve these creatures from extinction but possibly preserve her race as well or at least provide a means to seed other planets with our species, even if hybrid.

She knew without knowing that the new evolution, the planetary seeding, will include hundreds of thousands of people from Earth. There is a movement happening now, an awakening on Earth and at the time of the true end of days perhaps millions of others will be enlightened and ready for the journey to the next realm of existence, the next world.

Chapter Fourteen
The New Ones

⊕→

She knew without knowing that they could not take a part of her that could provide a life extension of herself without her agreement or before she had a child of her own.

The memories she has of the actual process are intermittent and some are actually comical. She recalls one dream in particular where numerous clones of a sperm donor were all walking in a line up what looked like a short stairwell. They were naked, with long curly red hair and chubby bodies like those you would imagine from the days of the ancient Roman empire. It reminded her of the story, *The Emperor's New Clothes* and she could help but laugh at loud at them. Thankfully their members were hidden by the large rolls of fat. If she had seen that she would have hit the floor laughing and that would have been rude. Although she has sketchy memory of some sexual manipulation and probing she does not recall intercourse; however she is certain of the experiment success because she has since met and interacted with the New Ones.

The New Ones are hybrids and unlike anything she has ever seen, excepting maybe some of the positive creatures from motion picture fantasy films. The New Ones are part human and part creature. Some have sprouts of hair-she never saw one with a full head of hair. They have beautifully brilliant color eyes that are the shape of a cat's eye. They are extremely intelligent and can process information in such a way that they are able to anticipate what your next thoughts are with accuracy. Like the Small Grays they are direct and to the point and pretty much force anyone communicating with them to do the same by moving the communication forward quickly, bypassing all the usual formalities and niceties of language as we know it. They have speech but their vocal range and sound pattern formation is either not the same as humans or they chose to use a dissimilar voice when communicating with her. The vocal range can best be described as similar to a music scale and similar to many humans, limited to the number of octaves found on a grand piano. The sounds when they form words sound like a blend of words and musical notes and chords. When they speak to her they speak slowly and use words sparingly. They are direct and to the point, do not include articles for the most part, phrasal prepositions, compound adjectives, correlative or subordinating conjunctions, adverbs or any word or phrase that would not be necessary to get a basic message across.

The New Ones are curious. They are just as curious as human children who want to explore, touch and taste everything they see. They behave very much like human children when they play, except they have early organized play, staying in groups-she does not recall ever seeing one play alone. The groups at play are eager to please, delight in positive reinforcement and look for reassurance just like a human child does only they react as a group and not individually.

One of their favorite activities without a doubt is singing. That was the first thing they wanted to do with her each time she saw them. She taught them a few camp songs, some early learning development songs and a few holiday favorites-They especially like 'Jingle Bells'. They have also created a few of their own, mostly by mixing up some of the lyrics and melodies of the songs they learned, but the result is pretty darn funny. She can't be certain but thinks this is their way of showing her their humor. It makes her laugh every time and they jump up and down when she does.

When they sing they sometimes skip certain words even if those words are included in the song lyrics. She found similarities to the way they communicate with the way a toddler communicates when first learning to talk, speaking only the essential words or using sign language to get a message across. She saw that the New Ones sometimes use a form of sign language similar to American Sign Language when they communicate in small groups or if one or two of them address a larger group.

The New Ones can also communicate with their eyes in a similar way humans do, by making them wider and more intense to express excitement for example. That their eyes contain cones (photoreceptors) may or may not be a byproduct of their hybrid status but the appearance of their eyes certainly make them look more human. They can also control the iris around their wide pupils in such a way that it seems they emit a tiny photon barely visible, but you know you saw something there. When she first witnessed this it reminded her of the night communication she experienced when sections of the night sky flashed in different light patterns.

Amid the many things that make the New Ones extraordinary is their ability to act and react in unison. It as though they are all connected by some invisible thought process. The first time she noticed this aside from their play was when she asked them to sing songs for her. In an instant they started to sing in unison, without any preamble of decision making. They just did it and did it precisely at the same time and in harmony. She heard them in her mind but the sound was as clear as she was witnessing a live choir performance.

When they collectively engage in some activity they can create a universal stream of consciousness to produce an energy wave powerful enough to light up a dark sky. It looks similar to the phenomenon commonly referred to as heat lightning. They can also project a wave individually as one or more colors. This is similar to the color aura around humans;

however, instead of a glow or hue around their body they project a narrow and precisely channeled beam of light. They can split and project their own aura from a brilliant white to dancing color like they are filtering it through a prism; however they have the added capability to enhance different color waves at will. Perhaps they just pull the color from our memory. When singing in unison their aura appears to originate from somewhere between the 6th Chakra, which is between the brow at the location of the third eye or pineal gland in humans to the 7th chakra which is at the top of the head.

She was not surprised that the New Ones showed a fondness for color because the world the Grays showed her was pretty much void of color variety and the color she remembers seeing was drab and dull, not unlike that found in a barren desert. Thinking of this reminds her of when she once traveled to a place where she assumed some Grays resided. In the light of day while gliding near ground level past a long rock-like formation she could see them standing in front of periodic openings that appeared in the rock. It reminded her of the Flintstones cartoon but without any color. She believes that they use color in part because they are now genetically engineered to express preference and creativity and in part as a way to bond with the humans they interact. Perhaps they are aware that exposure to different color is believed to play a part in human emotional response to a given situation.

According to color specialist Leatrice Eiseman, we relate color to how we perceive it in nature. The color blue for example is associated with clear skies so has a calming affect on people. The color green produces little eyestrain so a color scheme of blue and green is a good choice for a stressful environment, like an office. Black is considered an aggressive color and statistics from over 52,000 National Hockey League games show that the teams wearing black were penalized more for aggressive behavior.

In London, England, Angela Wright of Colour Affects writes that the length of the color wave plays a part in our perception. Red, for instance has the longest wave and appears nearer than it actually is and therefore captures our attention faster than other colors. It is no surprise then that the color for a traffic light is red the world over.

Chromotherapy-light therapy or colourology was practiced in Chinese and Egyptian ancient cultures and is still practiced as holistic treatment today according to Psychology Expert Kendra Cherry. In this treatment described by Cherry, "Red was used to stimulate the body and mind and increase circulation, Yellow to stimulate the nerves and purify the body, Orange to heal the lungs and to increase energy levels, Blue to soothe illnesses and treat pain, and Indigo to alleviate skin problems." Although chromotherapy is viewed with skepticism Cherry refers to studies that indicate color can have an impact on behavior. The installation of blue colored street lights can lead to a reduction of crime and the color red causes people to act with more speed and force. Cherry concludes that the influence color has on our emotional state and actions depends on "personal, cultural, and situational factors." Maybe that's why colors can be positive and negative. Blue can be calming or cold, Yellow optimistic or fearful, etc.

The New Ones express creativity using color and geometric symbols. They create art collaboratively, each piece a unified expression of some defined moment for them-an expression of an epiphany. In one of her dreams she was presented with a gift of their artwork. At the time of this particular visit they seemed the equivalent of three year olds but they appeared much younger, probably because of their size. As it was handed to her the New One said the word, "Ma." This was not unusual to hear because like most human toddlers call a woman authority figure Mom, regardless of the relationship, this group of New Ones called her Ma. She was genuinely touched by the gesture and remembers thinking that she wanted to give them additional art tools as a way of expressing her gratitude and encouraging their creativity. The art piece was a collage type picture sketch of various patterns drawn in their collective colors and significantly the first physical item she remembers attempting to bring back from a visit. She also remembers that the piece was confiscated at a transport site. It was taken from her without any explanation other that it was sensitive material and she felt she was reproached for her attempt to keep it by arguing ownership.

Chapter Fifteen
Nine Lives

ӡɑ꜀

How do you define and measure courage? Stories of bravery usually involve some self-less act to benefit another but that puts the actor in some sort of danger. What about courage on a more personal level? Should we consider risk taking courageous or is that just reckless behavior or thrill seeking? Are people who play it safe in life cautious or spine-less? Should we categorize acts of courage in relation to the individual experience? If we do, would repeated experiences of an extraordinary nature condition that person for bravery on a level tailored for just that person? If we accept that line of reasoning, should we also accept that what is brave for one person may be just ordinary for another? If an individual is repeatedly exposed to a particular stimuli will he/she be de-sensitized to its affects? Ever hear someone say, "It's all what you get used to?" She did and knew without knowing that her experiences with the Grays conditioned her for a strong self-confidence that allowed her to react at times without hesita-tion, to transform fear into rational thought, to avoid fixating on past negative events, and most importantly, to be ever op-timistic about the future regardless of the number of disap-pointing setbacks she endured. Perhaps she had just learned to pay attention to her inner instinct or intuition. Perhaps it was something more.

Most people experience situations in their lifetime that are close calls of one sort or another. Like that time when you were running late because you could not find your car keys or something else caused a few minutes delay in your routine.

You get on the freeway and just ahead there is a horrific accident. Or that time you decided at the last minute not to follow through with plans then learned later of a tragic happening at the event you would have attended. Or even more incredible that time when you were in a situation where you survived or were unhurt in some way against all odds. What force is working here? Is it just plain luck? Or is there something more behind this? She once worked with a woman who had strong intuitive feelings and on numerous occasions they involved other people she worked with. The woman would suddenly tell an employee not to leave work yet and we would later learn of a car accident on the regular route taken by that employee. The woman said it was spooky for her-It was spooky for us too, but after the first time she was proved right, no one doubted her. Some people have an unexplainable gift of knowing. They just know.

She can recall a variety of happenings that included varying degrees of danger, and although there may not have been an overt act of bravery involved, these events worked to numb her sense of fear and trained her to react solely using her strong sense of instinct and intuition. Like a cat with nine lives she averted dire consequences sometimes by not much more than the grace of God.

One: she was swimming in the Atlantic Ocean off the shores of Boca Raton, Florida. While at the beach, she enjoyed jumping the surf and body surfing at the breakwater. She was never an avid swimmer but was able to stay afloat well enough and enjoyed swimming on her back or treading water. She never mastered the art of the side to side head turn while mouth breathing and preferred to swim on her back or her side if her head was to touch the water. While she and several others enjoyed the refreshing surf she suddenly found that she was being carried out on a fast current. Rip tide! She knew better than to try and swim against it and instead let it carry her further out while she made her way through it. She steered her body as much to her right as she could while she swam freestyle with her head out of water, bobbing to the right and left as the rip carried her out further. Once she was out of the rip she tread water and looked back to shore to find she was pretty far out. She was farther out than she had ever been without a boat nearby. A panicky first thought shook her-what about sharks? She glanced around-no fins! Then another-what about underneath? How deep is the water? She had a sick to her stomach feeling of panic and fear. She started making her way back and just at the time she was beginning to doubt her ability to get back she felt a rush of adrenaline. She still swam with her head above water and as her head bobbed to the right she noticed a man swimming with his young daughter. They had also been caught in the same rip. She began to focus on the young girl thinking that she would help her if needed. They all three continued their efforts back to shore and the focus she had on the young girl took her mind off her wavering faith in her own ability and in her underlying fear that sharks could be lurking nearby. She no longer felt the strength draining from her arms but rather felt a renewed energy. It was as though the three of them had an invisible line that tied them and pulled them toward shore. Once they hit the break waters the waves propelled them in and they were all safely ashore where they exchanged happy grins before parting ways.

Two: One summer Saturday morning she drove to her office to catch up on some work. As she parked her car she saw a pair of construction type workers exiting a utility truck and walk out of the parking garage and toward the building. The building was locked and you needed a key card to trigger the front door unless you had an inside contact to call. By the time she reached the front door the pair she saw was not in sight. For no reason in particular she was glad they were gone. She did not care for being alone at the office, especially on a

Saturday or Sunday. Maybe it was because her office was located on the twelfth floor and although the offices were secured behind locked doors in a common corridor, she knew from the regular emergency drills that descending the unlit and empty stairwell alone while carrying a briefcase and toting her purse in the event of an emergency would not be a fun experience.

During the week the building is rarely empty, even into the later evening hours. She often worked late along with numerous others on her floor and throughout the building. On a weeknight there were security guards on site but she rarely saw them on a Saturday or Sunday. Security was an extra, just like air conditioning. If you planned to work on the weekend it was necessary to arrange air conditioning ahead of time. Otherwise, in summer, because the windows could not be opened to circulate air the inside, the temperature was only tolerable until about noon. She had not arranged air because she had intended to stay for only a few hours and she had a pretty high tolerance for heat.

She hit her key card against the inside of the elevator and pushed her floor number, one of only a few her card was programed to access, a security feature added post September 11, 2001. If you entered the elevator without a card on an upper floor the elevator would not stop on any floor until reaching the lobby. If you entered from the lobby the elevator would not take you up to any floor without an access card. It was possible to enter a floor from the stairwell only if the access door was unlocked, with the exception of the ground floor exit-that door always pushed open from the inside to the outside, locking to the outside once closed.

Once inside her office, secured behind the locked door she proceeded to work through the stack of case files and correspondence on her desk. After about an hour she began to feel lightheaded. She had breakfast and it was only about 11:00, too early for lunch. She reached for a bottle of water and took in a large amount but found the water left a funny aftertaste in her mouth. She started to get a headache and then smelled an odor but was not sure of the source. Then she heard what sounded like someone trying to turn the door knob on the corridor door. This was followed by a steady knocking on the door. She did not get up to open it because she knew that anyone who should have access would have a key card. She tried to return to the stack of work but could not get the interruption door knocking out of her head. It nagged at her as the odor permeating her office grew more intense and she started to feel faint. She was no longer able to concentrate so turned off her computer, grabbed her briefcase and purse then pushed out through her office door into the corridor. There was no smell in the corridor and by the time the elevator arrived her head began to clear.

She later learned was that there was some work being done in the office beneath hers that included the use of toxic chemicals but never learned the identity of the door knocker.

Three: She lived in an area prone to seismic activity and experienced regular small quakes. Her office building was engineered to withstand a larger Earthquake-It was built on rollers. While working one morning an earthquake near Santa Barbara, California was felt all the way to the City of Orange where she sat at her desk, the window behind her. She heard a movement in the window blinds and an unsettling stretching sound as the glass panes in the window reacted to the strain of the building's back and forth movement which was in and of itself frightening. The room began to tilt and she found herself holding onto her desk while the building balanced on the rollers below. The unnerving thing about this was that she did not know how far the building could sway without tipping over. Could that even happen? After that morning and her staff's newly found interest in the location of the earthquake

104

readiness bin, a large trunk size container with supposedly enough provisions to last until rescue should they find themselves trapped, she met with her direct reports and gave them each a small transistor radio with a battery for their personalized earthquake kits they were all encouraged to make. She put one in hers too, along with the usual essentials, food, water, first aid kit, flashlight and reading material. She smiles as she recalls a colleague commenting that if he packed an emergency kit he would put in his favorite liquor and porn to read so he could enjoy his plight regardless of the outcome. Ha!

When she first moved west to work in Los Angeles, she was confused by the sight of people pushing small luggage around. She never saw anything like it. Are they all going to the airport? Are they carrying cameras in their cases and shooting city scenes? She had seen that on a news show once. An undercover reporter took a camera hidden in a small luggage bag into a convenience store to film what would happen if a lottery ticket winner had the clerk confirm the ticket. Would the clerk honestly tell the purchaser the ticket was a winner or say it was not in order to keep the winning ticket? The city was not filled with people filming. She was informed by a co-worker that post September 11, 2001, most commuters working in Los Angeles carried emergency provisions. This was similar to what people do back east during the winter season when they pack a bag of sand, some road salt, an extra blanket and water in their car to prepare for a sudden snow or ice storm.

She was once caught in a sudden winter storm, the kind that starts out as a mild blizzard and increases in magnitude due to a circular weather pattern that moves over a large body of water picking up moisture then dumping it on land-lake effect snow. She had driven in the steadily falling snow to the airport only to find upon her arrival that the flight was canceled. All departing flights were canceled and incoming flights were noted as delayed across the flight schedule board. The runways were icing over and the emergency equipment used to clear the snow and ice were all pulled to work on the few incoming runways still open. She learned from the radio while driving back home that the highway patrol started closing the major roads including the one she was on. The road was eerily deserted but for a patrol car, a local news truck and a sparse number of travelers who, like her, were trying to get to their exit before getting stranded or worse. She instructed her young daughter to take a nap, which she did immediately. Sometimes children just know to listen without hesitation. Perhaps it was the tenseness of her tone of voice that alerted her daughter of the importance of doing what she was told. She needed complete focus because she could no longer see the lines on the road. She judged where she was by staying in the fast disappearing tire treads left by a truck she was following and by looking from side to side at the landscape, though that too was quickly morphing into one white layer. If the truck veered off the road she would likely follow and that possibility stayed in the forefront of her thoughts as she continued on slowly but steadily until finally, after what seemed like a lifetime she reached her exit and navigated the side roads safely home.

Four: Ft. Desoto Park is a beautiful 1,136 acre waterfront beach and picnic area on five offshore keys in Pinellas County, Florida where you can swim from the main key to a smaller outer key during low tide. Most park visitors attempt the shore to island swim and those who reach the island are rewarded with a treasure of huge seashells and sand dollars littering the beaches.

She and several friends (including Butterfingers) were there for the day, picnicking, swimming, and playing frisbee in the sand. While others in their group were making the shore to island swim, she and two friends tossed a frisbee around the sandy picnic area. It was a warm sunny day and the park was not overly crowded. On her turn to catch the frisbee she ran hard not noticing the T-shape water pipe sticking out of the sand in front of her. The frisbee was overhead so she leaped up in the air to grasp the edge of the disc without realizing she was about to run into the pipe. She came down on an open edge of the pipe (the handles had been removed) and it split open her groan instantly. As she stumbled to the ground she saw the blood running down her leg and immediately felt ill.

At that moment while Butterfingers' older brother was walking the island, he heard a noise that sounded like a foghorn and it alerted him to return to the main shore. Her friends called for the lifeguards who in turn called for an ambulance then tended to her by putting pressure on her wound while she laid there looking up past the circle of heads above her to the sky and feeling a great chill. She was going into shock and could no longer feel pain. She continued to look up, following the instruction of the lifeguard to try and stay still. That was pretty easy since she began to lose feeling in her legs and arms. She stared at the sky and then saw them-Three seagulls circling overhead. They circled and while they circled they looked down at her. She could see their eyes on her as they circled and then she knew she would be fine. It was as though they spoke to her, reassuring her that she would be okay. As the others learned that the bridge to the park was stuck in the upright position and the ambulance unable to reach her she was beginning to feel better. As the others were told that a rescue boat was launched and on the way to transport her, she was thinking about the seagulls and particularly about *Jonathan Livingston Seagull*, a favorite read.

A normal 20 to 25 minute rescue turned into over an hour. She was taken by boat to a local hospital where they had a plastic surgeon on stand by. After her wound was cleaned and stitched she was told several times that she was extremely lucky because the pipe injury missed her femoral artery by just a shade. It cut deeply before and after the artery and for some reason it did not slice through it. It was as though the artery retracted deeper into her leg to avoid the pipe's cutting edge. Five: While on another car trip she was unexpectedly caught in blinding fog. She was traveling on Interstate 5 Northbound from Los Angeles to the Monterey Bay area in the dark early hours of the morning when suddenly, BOOM!-blinding fog so thick she could not see a thing! It was like the dream you have when you find yourself driving without control. Her heart pounded as she braked the car to a near stop, afraid she would either go off the road or rear-end another vehicle. Her fear mounted when she realized that mostly large trucks are traveling the road at this time of day and she could easily be rear-ended. She took a few deep breaths, telling herself to relax and not panic, then it occurred to her to put on her flasher lights-At least if someone was coming up from the rear they might see her lights. She crawled along the road that was thankfully straight, staying in the far right lane concentrating her focus on the side of the road to see the lines that were barely visible until she drove out the far side of the cloud bank.

She was rear-ended once and that was a terrifying experience. She was driving on a Route 60 near the Pittsburgh International Airport when some joker stopped short in the far left hand lane to watch a car fire across the medium and in a lane moving in the opposite direction. Stopped short like it was a vista view! There was a limousine in front of her and it also stopped short! No! Not going to hit a limousine! She carefully stopped her car about a foot or two from the limo and breathed a sigh of relief. Her relief was short lived when she looked into her rear-view mirror to see a fast approaching car. She knew she would be hit so she put her foot on the brake, covered her head and waited for impact. Crash! It hit her right rear bumper after trying to avoid her too late. The hit moved her car forward and into the back of the limo-Crunch! Then another car came by, hitting the car behind her and then swerving into the right rear passenger side of her car. Even after thirteen years she finds herself anxiously peering into her rearview mirror any time traffic forces her to a sudden stop.

Six: Another intense driving episode occurred while she was living near Pittsburgh and driving to work during morning rush hour traffic. She had exited a tunnel and onto one of the many bridges crossing the rivers that surrounded the city. She found that she was in the wrong lane, too far to the right and if she remained in that lane she would exit to a transition road that headed east. She looked in her side mirror for a break in the traffic, put her blinker on and waited for the opportunity to merge left. She was about to execute the turn when a large semitrailer truck merged right, cutting her off. She slammed on her brakes as she watched in horror while the truck headed right for the front of her car. She was about to be hit and there was nothing she could do about it but wait for the inevitable impact. She gritted her teeth and just when the impact should have occurred she witnessed what looked like a portion of the truck moving through the front bumper of her car. The right portion of the truck appeared transparent as she watched it move right through the car and off to the right, down the transition exit ramp. It must have been as close as it could possibly have been without actually touching her car. So close that it appeared to be on top of her as it passed by. After it passed she found herself stopped in the middle of a small triangular section of roadway between the transition ramp exit and the other lanes of traffic. She was facing a traffic barrel placed at the tip of the triangle. It was a miracle the truck did not take out her car, the barrel, and part of the concrete barrier.

Seven: A strange event occurred while she was on board a 747 airplane. At that point in her career she was living in California and traveling quite a bit, attending depositions, mediations and making court appearances. On one such occasion she was traveling from the West coast to the East coast on an itinerary that included a landing in Newark New Jersey. During the flight the pilot received word of delays at the Newark airport due to severe thunderstorms in the area. He was given directive to fly in a circular pattern while they were somewhere over Pennsylvania. Some of the passengers noticed that the plane was going in circles and asked the stewardess why. Around this same time the pilot came on the speaker system and in a steady matter-of-fact tone of voice informed the passengers he had the plane in a circular holding pattern due to severe weather occurring along the East coast. He proceeded to add that there was an additional problem-the plane was running low on fuel and it did not appear that they had enough fuel to make it to Newark. Did he just say what she thought he said? She turned from looking out the window to looking left, searching the faces of nearby passengers trying to find some validation of what she thought she heard the pilot say. She saw another passenger sitting up one row and in the far left window seat turn around to his right and look her square in the eye. Yes, his expression told her, you heard right. What happened over the next hour or so was amazing.

First, there was no panic whatsoever. Everyone remained as calm as can be-She thought the majority of them must not have understood the seriousness of the situation because no one was even talking about it, at least not that she could hear. She felt pretty calm too though, considering the circumstances and quickly resigned herself to the fact that there was nothing she could do but be consciously positive. What the pilot did next was remarkable to her because she had never experienced it and had no idea it could be done. He brought the plane out of the holding pattern and was once again traveling in an Easterly direction, steadily dropping altitude as the plane moved forward, like when approaching for landing, only they were not close enough to Newark to land. As they continued the journey he dropped the plane lower and lower until at one point she could see the tree tops as they glided overhead. A thought crossed her mind-Those tree tops look soft enough to land on. What? Did she actually think they could land on the trees? It was then that the lady sitting next to her turned to her and said, "These planes can glide quite a long distance." Oh, so that was it! The plane was gliding all the way to Newark? Was that even possible?

She had never heard of a commercial airliner gliding but there are documented cases of such happenings. CBC News reported Air Canada Flight 143 Boing 767-233 Gimli commercial jet that landed safely on July 23, 1983, after running out of fuel in midair. CBC News Canada reported that the captain and his first officer glided the jet and its 69 passengers and crew to a safe landing at a decommissioned runway located on an air force base where a crowd was watching go cart races. That jet is now known as the Gimli glider.

How far can a commercial jet glide? According to a posting on message board straightdope.com a 747 has a glide ratio of about 17:1 meaning it can travel 17 feet forward for every foot lost in altitude. So if a plane was traveling at 35,000 feet and lost all engine power it could glide approximately 110 miles before landing. If the pilot tries to maintain altitude the fuel consumption is huge so the best course of action is to bring the plane down low which is what the pilot did on her flight. The plane she was on continued to glide for what seemed like an eternity and at one point she felt that the plane was holding up through the force of their will alone. They must have been nearly out of fuel and yet were still up in the air gliding along. The pilot came on the speaker again to inform the passengers that he had clearance to land and refuel at a nearby military base. That pilot-the best pilot in the world-glided the plane safely to the base and as it taxied along a runway she could see several other commercial planes scattered around the landing field. Once on the ground the passengers were instructed to remain seated and informed that they could not deplane; however one man seated several rows behind her would not comply. He insisted on standing and said he wanted to get off the plane. A short time later a couple of uniformed military men boarded the plane and removed him. When they finally arrived, she never thought she could be so happy to see Newark.

Eight: Sometimes the brain takes over in the flight or fight mode and the body reacts appropriately. She had this experience one evening while getting ready for bed. She had showered and washed her hair and was drying her hair with a blow dryer in the bathroom when suddenly the lights went out. She immediately thought she had overloaded the fuse so went to locate the fuse box which was on the outside of the small efficiency apartment serving as her temporary housing. She found the box quick enough, opened it then reset all the switches. As she did so she saw the lights flick back on. When she returned to the bathroom she heard a funny gurgling sound. The blowdryer had fallen into the commode. It seemed that she had neglected to turn off the power switch when she left to reset the fuses and the surge of new electric current caused a vibration sufficient to bounce the blowdryer from the sink's edge down into the toilet. When she saw it in the water she almost reached in to grab it but something stopped her. Her arm recoiled backward and she pulled the plug from the wall socket instead. The action was instant and without thought. She just did it.

Nine: The strangest incident occurred later in the evening on that same Saturday she was working in her office. She was sleeping at the apartment complex where she rented a split plan two bedroom two bath unit. There had been some reports of car vandalism-her downstairs neighbor's vehicle was keyed, as was hers-and a few unit break-ins. It was late, well after midnight, and she was asleep when she was suddenly jarred awake by a sound coming from the patio. It sounded like the scraping of a chair against the wooden deck floor. Her bedroom was closest to the front door and beyond that the dining alcove area that had a sliding glass door opening to a patio that ran width of the living room. At the opposite end of the patio was a second slider opening into the second bedroom. Her daughter was visiting her Dad out of town so she knew that she was not the source of the noise. She sat up alert for more sound and thought it may be that cat that was always jumping on her patio. Maybe the cat lunged onto the chair causing the sound. The door to her bedroom was open and she could see the verticals on the dining area patio door but they were closed so she could not see the outside. She was about to get out of bed to investigate when she saw several Tall Grays, one that stepped in front of the entrance to her room and beyond, two more standing in the dining area near the vertical blinds. The one in the doorway took a step toward her and gestured for her to remain where she was. The Tall Gray then turned toward the patio and gestured for her to look. When she looked she could see, incredibly, through the blinds and out onto the patio where two men were standing. She should have been terrified but she only stared in disbelief. At this point she had a clear understanding that these creatures were there to protect her and that she did not need to worry or fear anything. She laid back down to sleep and totally forgot the dream until long after she had moved out of the apartment.

She knew that the reason she was not afraid of the Tall Grays the night she dreamed them in her apartment was because it was not the first time she encountered them. She could never forget the first time she interacted with the Tall Grays because the first time she interacted with them they were extremely annoying. She could never forget the first time for

113

one other more important reason. She could never forget her first time interacting with the Tall Grays because it was also the first time she saw the moon roll.

Chapter Sixteen
The Rolling Moon

Planet Earth spins round on its ever slightly shifting axis once in approximately 24 hours and rotates 100 times faster than its moon. The Earth's moon orbits the Earth once every 27.3 days which is about the same time it takes to rotate on its axis, so we always see its same side; however due to its elliptical orbit, we can actually see 59 percent of the surface when it slows down at the farthest point from Earth. The lunar moon cycle (new moon to new moon) takes 29.5 days, so to account for the difference of days in the monthly Gregorian Calendar there is a second moon that occurs in a monthly lunar cycle approximately every three years. This second moon is referred to as a blue moon. There were blue moons in November 2001, July 2004, June 2007, December 2009, August 2012, and another projected for July 2015. It was on such an occasion that she traveled to a place where she encountered both Small and Tall Grays and witnessed a remarkable change in the moon.

A few additional words about the Grays: The Small and Tall Grays are likely a related species even though they have many physical differences. Considering the similarities in their outward appearances-color, and eye shape to name two-one could speculate that they share some cosmic ancestry. One could also speculate that humans share this same ancestry because we are all made up of cosmic dust. If we consider the differences in features between humans residing on Earth's seven continents it is not too hard to imagine an alien species with varying features among them.

The ones called Small Grays (nicknamed 'Kinderrmen' or 'kind to men') are shorter than the average human female, about four and a half to five feet and they walk around with all the air and authority that one would imagine held by a scientist working in a laboratory or a doctor in a university lecture hall. They are the color of water reflecting a clouded sky in the midmorning or a foggy sky, not yet blue, but an illuminated very light grey and as written earlier, very cool to the touch. Their legs and arms are thin and arms disproportionately longer as their legs are shorter, to the rest of their body. Their eyes are large, upwardly slanted, deep black and mesmerizing to a stare. It is best, she mused, never to look a Small Gray directly in the eye if you can avoid it.

She recalls staring into the eyes of a Small Gray one moment then finding herself in another place entirely in what seemed like an instant. The Small Gray was no longer facing her and she had no recollection of what occurred. The surroundings had changed and she knew without knowing that they had traveled some far distance. She had heard stories about blackouts from a recovering alcoholic she had once worked with. He shared that he drank so much that he blacked out in one place and awoke in another country without any recollection of how he got there. What happened to her when she looked into a Small Gray's eyes can be described similarly, except at the time it happened she was not drinking or using any kind of drug.

The Tall Grays (nicknamed 'Zook') were much different. Their color was not illuminating but still a fairly light shade of grey in the daylight. At night they were darker, almost the color of shadowy grey. They walked like shadows in the night. Tall Grays were tall and lanky with arms and legs proportionate to the rest of their body. The easily fit in the space behind a tree, even a thin one and that was their favorite spots to hide during the night. Their heads though, were small-

116

er, much smaller than the Small Gray, and from a side view it appeared almost flat on top. Unlike Small Grays, Tall Grays had a discernible jaw and a mouth that reminded her of what her father's looked like when he did not have his false teeth in place.

Their behavior differed as well. While the Small Gray was authoritative, reserved, and acted purposely, at times the Tall Grays acted with abandon, like mischievous adolescents. They would jump up and down at each other and release what she could only describe as a laugh. The sound was not the contagious kind of laughter one hears and cannot help but smile or join in on if engaged closely with the one laughing. Nor was it of the sort one would describe as a nervous laugh. This sound was different from any she had heard, yet had some familiarity to it, like when you hear something and can't quite put your finger on what it is. The sound Tall Grays made while acting out was a high pitched type of cackle and just plain weird. The closest comparison she can think of is a combination of zebra, locust, and the chirp of a bird.

She believed that Tall Grays were tasked with security because whenever she encountered them they carried a very annoying small pistol like device that if unleashed on you caused a stinging sensation like being zapped with a light charge of electricity. She knows how it felt because she was caught in the crossfire the night she first witnessed the moon rolling.

She recalls detail of that night when she was standing near several Tall Grays that held little devices they used to zap each other while they jumped up and down in what appeared to be play. When they jumped their legs bent but almost sideways and they sprang up pretty high bringing the jointed portion of their legs up and outward. They took on the appearance of a praying mantis when they jumped and it might have been comical to watch if not for the hideous noise they made that overshadowed the entertaining value of the jumping. She watched several of them as they noisily jumped around. She was annoyed that they were fooling around like unruly children and she tried to ignore them but it was impossible as they moved closer to her still zapping each other with the device that was no larger than a medium size child's water pistol. The pistol-like device was not brightly colored but she could see it clearly from several yards away. Then, without warning they turned on her and she was part of their play. They started zapping her on the upper arm just below her right shoulder, jumping and laughing while doing so. The zapping was not painful. It felt like the static electric shock you get when you rub a balloon in your hair then touch someone. You know its coming but the shock is still surprising. She was mostly irritated. Maybe because she had no opportunity to zap them in return- that was unfair. Maybe it was because she was outnumbered or maybe she was just getting tired of hearing them make noise that began to sound like constant teasing. She let them know she was not amused, gave them a harsh look and shouted "Hey, stop it!" They immediately stopped. At first she thought they were listening to her and she was caught off guard, like when your child promptly does what you ask when you least expect it, but she soon learned better when she turned in the direction of their attention and saw a Small Gray approaching. Later she realized that the tiny shocks she received were just part of their play. That they were at play, that they played at all was totally lost on her at the time because she was caught up in her own emotions. So the Tall Grays engage in play-pretty incredible!

When the Small Gray reached them it gestured up at the blue moon brilliant and hanging in the night sky. They were all standing on a flattened barren hilltop not close enough to the rounded end to see what, if anything was below. She had no recollection of how she got to this place but that

118

was typical of these encounters or perhaps just typical of what she remembered when she awoke. She knew she was there and able to remember for a specific reason because the Small Grays never took her anywhere or showed her anything haphazardly. They always acted purposely and without hesitation. She also knew she did not have any real choice in the situation. It wouldn't have made a difference regardless because if she had had a choice she would have chosen to stay in that moment. A puzzling but true fact was that she actually trusted the Small Grays. Maybe the trust developed over the many years of encountering Small Grays who always, without exception acted exactly as they indicated they would. There was something more though. She had a distinct feeling that they trusted her in return. There was an exchange of trust between them that is usually part of a friendship or bond that develops between people who interact over a long period of time. She can't explain it any other way. It just is what it is. So as she stood there on that hilltop she waited patiently and without question.

Then it started. She noticed some movement out of her left peripheral line of vision. It was the moon. The moon began to move. The movement was not the same as she had noticed during clear nights on Earth, when one can intermittently see the moon shift in the night sky from the West to the East. The daily rise and fall of the moon happens slowly over the course of several hours. The moon was not rising or falling now. It was moving at a visible rate and coming closer to where she stood, her eyes transfixed on the giant orb. As it moved in closer it began to lob and roll forward toward them like a giant glowing bowling ball moving through the sky. As suddenly as it started to move it stopped then turned slightly left. She stood motionless, frozen, unable to move her feet. It was as though her feet were glued to the underlying dirt. Suddenly she detected a discernible change in the moon. Though

119

still very full, the appearance had changed. She searched for detail that would explain the change. It was as though a picture on a screen was suddenly replaced with another that was nearly exact as the first but not quite-something was different. That's it-the curve of the moon was not the same! As she stared at the giant orb she could see the outline of what looked like a seam running along its far right curve. At first she had to strain to see it because it blended so well with the night sky but it was there. It reminded her of the mark of the equator on a table-top globe, only this line appeared on the side of the moon. As she stood staring, still unable to move, the line began to widen. As the black thickness of the line grew wider she saw that the fullness of the moon's glow lessened slightly as the moon shifted further to the left.

As she stood there watching the shifting moon she detected the outline of a hinge. In the shadowed edge of the moon where it met the night sky there was definitely a hinge. The moon was hinged and it was opening. The lighted moon continued to wane as the curve opened further while it rolled to the left, widening the opening to a larger, deeper darkness. Then it hit her. Her heart beat faster, not with fear, but with excited anticipation as she realized they would be transported inside.

Epilogue

ω

Lucid dreaming is a phenomenon of sleep that occurs when you are aware you are dreaming while in a dream. When in the state of lucid dreaming, believed to occur during REM sleep, the dreamer can direct the events and overcome fears or live out fantasies.

There are two known ways lucid dreaming begins. The first is by some abnormal occurrence in a dream that shakes the dreamer into realizing he or she is in a dream state. The second is after a brief waking state, where the dreamer falls asleep again and into the same dream.

As recounted throughout these pages she experienced lucid dreams in both ways described and could normally re-count some detail when she awoke.

When she was young she had several recurring night-marish dreams that repeated until, while dreaming lucidly she was able to direct herself to face her fear while in the dream. She was always running from something terrifying, on the basement stairs of her house unable to get to the top or on her neighborhood street waking up just before being overrun by her pursuer. Through dreaming she was able to stop short of the waking point and turn around to face whatever was there and upon doing so found there was nothing there! Bam! That was the end of the recurring nightmare.

Most people have at least one lucid dream in their life-time while others are able to lucidly dream on a regular basis. While in the lucid dream, the dreamer's neuronal activity is equivalent to actually perceiving or doing what takes place in the dream and therefore it is not unusual to mistake a lucid dream for reality.

That is the best explanation she has, at least for now.

References

12 Nov. 2014 "How many solar systems are in our galaxy?" <http://www.spaceplace.nasa.gov>

3 Nov. 2014 <http://www.dictionary.reference.combrowse/normal>; <http://www.meriam-webster.com/dictionary/normal>

LaBerge, Stephen, Ph.D., "Lucid Dreaming: Psychophysiological Studies of Consciousness during REM Sleep." 25 Oct. 2014 <http://www.lucidity.com/SleepAndCognition.html>

"Woodstock." Page last modified on 14 Oct. 2014. Accessed 14 Oct. 2014 <http://en.wikipedia.org/wiki/Woodstock>

This Day in History "17 Aug. 1969: Woodstock Music Festival concludes." 14 Oct. 2014 <http://www.history.com/this-day-in-history/woodstock-music-festival-concludes>

Tingen, Paul, "Using Mindfulness to Rewire the Brain . . . ". 2012. 14 Oct. 2014 <http://www.mindfulnessbell.org/wp/2012/10/using-mindfulness-to-rewire-the-brain/>

Carr, Nicholas. The Shallows: What the Internet is Doing to Our Brains. W. W. Norton and Company, 2010.

DavidJi,"Awaken Your Creativity; Gratitude Meditation; Healing Meditation; Dream Meditation; Third Chakra Meditation." Chopra Centered Lifestyle 3 Sept. 2014 <http://http://www.chopra.com/ccl/guided-meditations>

Bancarzl, Steven, "Silva Mind Control." 3 Sept. 2014 <http://spiritscienceandmetaphysics.com>

Klein, Dr. David, "Pineal Gland and retinal photoreceptors." 25 Sept. 2012. 3 Sept. 2014 <http://consiouslifenews.com>

Edwards, Debbie, "The Peizolectric Effect and the Pineal Gland in the Human Brain." 22 Oct. 2014 <https://physics.-knoji.com/the-piezoelectric-effect-and-the-pineal-gland-in-the-human-brain/>

"How to Decalcify Your Pineal Gland." 3 Sept. 2014 <http://UTube> and <http://www.spiritscienceandmetaphysics.com/proof-that-the-pineal-gland-is-literally-a-3rd-eye/>

"Opening the Pineal Gland/Third Eye." 1 Sept. 2013. 3 Sept. 2014 <http://consiouslifenews.com>

Layton, Julia, "How Fear Works." 22 Sept. 2014 <http://science.howstuffworks.com/life/inside-the-mind/emotions/fear2.htm>

Dobson, James "Fatal Addiction: Ted Bundy's Final Interview." 14 Oct. 2014 <http://www.pureintimacy.org/f/fatal-addiction-ted-bundys-final-interview/>

Montaldo, Charles, "Serial Killer Ted Bundy." 14 Oct. 2014 <http://crime.about.com/od/serial/p/tedbundy.htm>

Kuhnke, Elizabeth, Body Language for Dummies. John Wiley & daughters LTD, Chichester, West Sussex, England, 2007.

Radford, Benjamin, "Astral Projection: Just a Mind Trip." 18 Mar. 2001. 3 Oct. 2014 <http:www.BenjaminRadford.com>

Güijosa, Alberto, "What is String Theory?" 4 Sept. 2009. 3 Oct. 2014 <http://www.nuclecu.unam.mx/~alberto/physics/string.html>

Ly, John, Administrator, "Working with telluric energy." 22 Sept. 2014 <http://myspiritualgroup.com>

"The Human Body Energy System - Aura & Chakras", 14 Oct. 2014 <http://desertstarhealing.com/tag/auric-body-system/>

Eiseman, Leatrice, "Ten Ways Color Affects Your Mood." 9 Oct. 2014 <http://www.scienceofpeople.com/2013/01/10-ways-color-affects-your-mood/>

Wright, Angela, "Psychological Properties of Colour." 9 Oct. 2014 <http://www.colour-affects.co.uk/psychological-proper-ties-of-colour>

Cherry, Kendra, "How Colors Impact Moods, Feelings, and Behaviors." 9 Oct. 2014 <http://psychology.about.com/od/sensationandperception/a/colorpsych.htm>

Cooper, Kim and CJ Kazilek, "Seeing Color." 17 Dec. 2009. 29 Sept. 2014 <http://askabiologist.asu.edu/colores-they-see>

Tyson, Jeff, "How Night Vision Works." 27 Apr. 2001. 3 Oct. 2014 < http://electronics.howstuffworks.com/gadgets/high-tech-gadgets/nightvision.htm>

"Flying on empty: 5 Harrowing gliding incidents, Heroic landings of commercial jets after running out of fuel-with no lives lost." 3 Oct. 2014 <http://www.cbc.ca/news2/interactives/gliders/>

Phlosphr,"Can a 777 or a 747 airliner Glide? If so how far?" 6 May 2003 Shagnasty response 6 May 2003 <http:/www.s-traightdope.com/sdmb/showthread.php?t=182160>

"Moon Phases.", Stardate On Line. 17 Sept. 2014 <http://stardate.org/nightsky/moon>

www.ingramcontent.com/pod-product-compliance
Lightning Source LLC
Chambersburg PA
CBHW050528280326
41933CB00011B/1506